Poverty and Freedom

CASE STUDIES ON GLOBAL
ECONOMIC DEVELOPMENT

Poverty and Freedom

CASE STUDIES ON GLOBAL ECONOMIC DEVELOPMENT

EDITED BY MATT WARNER

Atlas Economic Research Foundation
Arlington, VA

Poverty and Freedom: Case Studies on Global Economic Development

Copyright © 2019 by Atlas Economic Research Foundation.

Edited by Matt Warner.
Co-edited by Melissa Mann, Casey Pifer, and A. J. Skiera.
Editing and production support by David Lampo.
Cover photo by Bernat Parera.
Cover design by Meredith Reshoft of Killswitch Collective.

ISBN: 978-0-578-55754-0
Ebook ISBN: 978-1-7923-1668-5
Library of Congress Control Number: 2019913591
Library of Congress Cataloguing-in-Publication Data available.

Atlas Network
Two Liberty Center
4075 Wilson Blvd.
Suite 310
Arlington, VA 22203
www.atlasnetwork.org

"Mostly in the world there are not poor people. There are people living in poor places."
—Lant Pritchett, Harvard University

"The secret to modernity is that we collectively use large volumes of knowledge, while each one of us holds only a few bits of it."
—Ricardo Hausmann, *The Atlas of Economic Complexity*

"Wealth is knowledge and its origin is evolution."
—Eric Beinhocker, *The Origin of Wealth*

"Even if a narrow, simplistic, mechanistic, reductionist form of global altruism is our legacy, it needn't be our fate."
—Ben Ramalingam, *Aid on the Edge of Chaos*

Acknowledgments

The Atlas Network team would like to thank the John Templeton Foundation and the Smith Family Foundation for their generous support which made this publication possible. We would also like to thank the independent think tanks in our network whose vision, leadership, and innovative work are responsible for all the successes highlighted in this book. The primary purpose of this publication is to showcase their work, disseminate innovative ideas, and encourage a stronger network of leaders around the world promoting economic freedom in pursuit of poverty reduction.

Atlas Network also thanks Chip Bishop, Hilary Gowins, and other freelance contributors for their help preparing case study materials.

Contents

Introduction: A New Approach to Poverty
By Matt Warner

In the 1800s, the U.S. Forest Service began observing a strict, zero-tolerance policy toward forest fires, believing that proper care of nature meant stopping anything from dying by flame. We have since learned that small fires in a forest actually play an important role in preventing larger, more catastrophic fires because, in part, they clear away old growth in manageable doses. By introducing interventions like small fire prevention, forest experts managed to achieve the very opposite of their aim, leaving forests much more vulnerable.[1]

When it comes to doing good by intervention, this kind of linear thinking can be hard to resist. We continue, for example, to think that the way to end poverty is to transfer wealth and expertise from one place to another. Some places are rich and educated. Some places are not. Take from one and give to the other. There's a simplicity to this thinking that appeals to our sense of moral urgency but it foolishly underestimates the complexity of the ecosystems we hope to see thrive.[2]

As a result, poor places become more vulnerable to permanent poverty. In the same way that small fires allow forests to reorient themselves for new growth, unfettered economies allow communities to reorient themselves over time toward new, sustainable development. In this iterative process, they make themselves less susceptible to catastrophic events.

Given this complexity, the challenge is how to help from the outside without making things worse. What *can* we do to help?

Rethinking Our Role

Mauricio Miller won the MacArthur Genius grant in 2012 for his radical rethinking of poverty. Up to that point, he spent 35 years in

Oakland, California, working with a traditional, transfer-based aid model for low-income populations until he started to realize that, as he puts it, "most of what [we] believe about poverty is wrong."[3]

In his recent book, he writes, "Government and private philanthropy are good at talking and planning, but . . . they never consider the possibility that their top-down solutions and plans will never solve poverty or create economic mobility."[4]

For Miller, the big mistake we make as outsiders is overstepping. We falsely believe our own knowledge and resources represent the bulk of what is needed to solve long-term economic problems on behalf of others and so, despite good intentions, we tend to assume far too much of a leadership role in their affairs.

Miller believes that at the heart of this tendency is our failure to take the idea of human dignity seriously enough. It is our failure to see that those who live in poverty are neither our victims nor our charges, dependent on us to save them. They are our equals—and his key message is that *they* are the rightful leaders when it comes to figuring out how to improve their lives, not the outsiders who are trying to help them.

For Miller, that assertion is no bromide. He has radically changed the way he and his team approach poverty. Instead of providing his clients free services, he champions their own individualized initiatives to get ahead. And he restrains himself and his staff from interfering when they think they know better. In fact, he has one rule for his staff: *If you help a low-income client, you're fired.*

Miller recognizes that the best solutions to poverty are context-sensitive and specific to the individual, part of a more complex and idiosyncratic landscape of social and economic choices. This means their knowledge and perspective make them the best equipped, using their own values and judgment, to navigate a path to prosperity. To give them the best chance to succeed, he suggests we stop focusing on what we provide those in poverty and consider more critically how we might be limiting their agency within a landscape of personal and economic opportunity.

Oxfam expert Duncan Green in his book, *How Change Happens*, describes this landscape of choices as the "enabling environment"

2

for individual initiative, and he stresses that empowering those in poverty means placing their actions center stage, not ours.[5]

The Power of Agency, Networks, and "Positive Deviance"

A common criticism of any approach that prizes individual initiative is to point out that no one truly succeeds on their own—no man is an island—so it's wrong to expect those in poverty to solve their own problems. Much has been said and written about the "bootstrap myth"[6]—criticizing the idea that all low-income people need to do is pull themselves up by their bootstraps and solve their own problems. It's certainly true that social networks and social capital play an important role in achieving individual success in prosperous communities, and so, indeed, it would be a mistake to ignore this important fact when it comes to helping people in poverty.

However, Miller discovered a nuance that serves to reconcile the respective roles of individual initiative and social capital in poverty reduction. He learned that when trying to help people in poor places, *who* they rely on and the *nature* of those social ties make all the difference. Miller realized he and his team were actually undermining social ties in low-income communities by strengthening their ties to social service agencies and other outside, professional "experts." That dependency approach wasn't working, and it was sabotaging better alternatives.

The new approach he adopted, instead, was first pioneered by Jerry and Monique Sternin when they worked on the problem of infant malnutrition in Vietnam for the nonprofit foundation Save the Children in the 1990s. In their book, *The Power of Positive Deviance: How Unlikely Innovators Solve the World's Toughest Problems*, the Sternins explained that one of the mistakes we make when working on social problems is dismissing outliers as anomalies instead of recognizing that they likely hold the key to discovering a viable, local solution.[7]

In Vietnam, the Sternins decided to investigate why a tiny fraction of families among the low-income population were *not* experiencing infant malnutrition despite facing the same resource constraints as their neighbors. They discovered among the healthy families a variety of unique habits, some observed unknowingly, such as more frequent feedings and the use of unpopular ingredients.

Importantly, the Sternins didn't insert themselves as the new experts to teach those habits as "best practices" to the rest of the population. Green emphasizes the importance of this break from traditional habit when he warns, "if external experts investigate outliers and turn the results into a toolkit, little will come of it. When communities make the discovery for themselves behavioral change can take root providing what the authors [the Sternins] call social proof."[8]

To make that discovery more likely, the Sternins facilitated the natural diffusion of those habits by encouraging the healthy families to cook with their neighbors. In so doing, they facilitated the strengthening of local social ties. It paid off. Malnutrition dropped 65 to 80 percent in a population of 2.2 million. For those Vietnamese families, their problem was solved in the same way most problems are solved. Someone, somewhere inside the system discovered or stumbled on a viable solution, and the "fitness" of that solution led to its natural replication.

Evolution, Local Knowledge, and Economic Freedom

If this sounds a lot like evolution, it is. Economies and social networks are complex adaptive systems that scholars study just as they would all evolutionary phenomena. In fact, Oxford economist Eric Beinhocker explains that wealth—the goal of any poverty reduction strategy—must be a product of evolutionary processes.[9]

Evolutionary processes, such as those necessary for economic development in low-income places, are stymied, not helped, by attempts to manipulate or centrally design them. Instead, as evolutionary philosopher Daniel Dennett puts it, evolution is a search algorithm that "finds needles of good design in haystacks of possibility."[10] Like healthy markets, evolution is design without a designer, making progress a function of the cumulative results of simultaneous yet uncoordinated experiments performed by large numbers of connected individuals.

Solving the Outsider's Dilemma

For those who advocate increased economic freedom in poor places, there is much validation to be found in the work of thought leaders like Miller, Green, and the Sternins, whose conclusions about individual agency seem to strengthen the case for decentralization, even limited government. Whether they would see it that way is unclear. What is clear is there is a growing consensus among thoughtful and experienced aid, poverty, and economic development experts that cautions outsiders, broadly defined, to take care not to impose their ideas and plans on others, particularly on those most vulnerable to suffering by our mistakes. This brings further into focus the serious dilemma, "the outsider's dilemma," that any outsider must grapple with: how can we help without mistakenly doing more harm than good?

Atlas Network would like to see that consensus grow, and so we propose a set of modest principles designed to resolve that dilemma in a way that we hope transcends ideological diversity in the spirit of "Doing Development Differently."[11] Those principles are laid out below in this introduction and explored further in sections I and II of this book. To demonstrate the application of those principles in practice, sections III through VII offer illustrative case studies from a variety of countries including the United States. Taken together, we hope this book offers encouraging evidence of a viable, scalable solution to "the outsider's dilemma" in pursuit of global poverty reduction. Those foundational principles are:

Principle #1: Ensure outsiders are not substantively leading local change and recognize that governments, even domestic governments, often behave as outsiders when it comes to interfering with individual agency and choices.

It is actually very likely that even a small amount of outsider influence will distort the evolutionary search for local solutions.

For that reason, in 2005, the broader aid community in 161 countries tried to put a stop to prescriptive restraints on international aid dollars via an agreement known as the Paris Declaration on Aid Effectiveness.[12]

Despite best intentions, the agreement failed because governments in both donor and recipient countries continued to complicate development goals with political considerations. In a sense, this was inevitable. Governments, even domestic governments, can behave like outsiders, prone to distorting economic life.

Dayo Olopade, an American-Nigerian journalist who knows all too well the harms caused by aid in the region, explains in her book, *The Bright Continent: Breaking Rules and Making Change in Modern Africa*, that "One of the biggest problems with the world's longtime orientation toward Africa is a preference for interactions between governments, or between formal institutions, when the most vibrant, authentic, and economically significant interactions are between individuals and decentralized groups."[13]

Olopade's observation, when combined with Beinhocker's work on evolution and wealth, underscores the need for a new approach that is less dependent on governments to lead change. For the evolutionary process of local economies, even local government can be a distorting outsider, and hopelessly so when under the influence of a foreign government.

Principle #2: Support the vision of local, independent think tanks to achieve institutional change.

In our search for nongovernmental leadership at the systemic level, there is increasing recognition that local think tanks can play an outsized role. In a 2017 paper published in cooperation with the Hewlett Foundation's Think Tank Initiative, Guy Lodge and Will Paxton, founders of Kivu International, a nonprofit committed to locally led policy change, make the case that local think tanks represent an *undervalued* resource when it comes to global strategies for achieving relevant and lasting reform.[14]

In our observation at Atlas Network, over the last 20 years local, independent think tanks have become more influential throughout the world, both as a result of an increase in their numbers as well as an increase in their ability to identify and articulate systemic solutions for local problems. Specifically, think tanks are starting to have an outsized impact on creating new levels of economic opportunity for low-income populations.

Take, for example, the case study on land titling in South Africa highlighting the work of a local think tank, Free Market Foundation, headquartered in Johannesburg. After successfully supporting legislation to allow the title transfer of government-owned housing after the end of Apartheid, the think tank staff discovered that only a few of those eligible were taking advantage of the opportunity. Even after the Free Market Foundation hired lawyers to provide free legal aid to renters in low-income neighborhoods, the number of applicants were still low.

As it turned out, there was not enough trust in government or outsiders (big-city lawyers) and, consequently, most thought the offer was too good to be true. Only when Free Market Foundation staff hired local lawyers and worked with local employers did they succeed in accelerating property ownership and local demand for property rights.

Principle #3: Prioritize institutional increases in individual agency or economic freedom.

The third principle concerns the type of change that is needed at the systemic level: one that increases latitude for "individuals and decentralized groups" to iteratively explore and discover viable solutions to their problems as they've defined them. Research shows that both culture and economic freedom play an important role in achieving economic prosperity, but that economic freedom is the stronger predictor of success.[15]

You can read about Aimable Manikiraza's experience in Burundi, where the formal market was off-limits for most low-income merchants due to exorbitant business registration fees. This is one of the most common barriers to entry, as business registration fees impose at least three artificial costs on would-be formal market participants.

First, the published fee itself can be high, thus disproportionately preventing low-income businesses from participating in legal markets. Second, the business registration process is often overly complicated and requires too many government officials to approve. This can impose absurd delays and a high tax on an applicant's time, time few people with low incomes can afford to spare. Finally, all those government hurdles create opportunities for corruption, such as bribes.

In India, for example, one modest entrepreneur told the staff of the think tank Centre for Civil Society that he knew that if he were to register his business formally, he'd have to first save up an arbitrarily determined amount of reserves in the bank to qualify *and* he would have to provide the bureaucrat in charge a hefty bribe to approve the license. Faced with all of these unnecessary costs, many prospective entrepreneurs are effectively shut out of legal markets.

Other misguided policies can create perverse incentives for government agents, leading to unwelcome interference with or even the destruction of local businesses without legal cause. Groundbreaking research by the Institute for Justice in the United States, for example, showed how modest-sized enterprises can be irreversibly harmed by the practice of civil asset forfeiture which allows the police to confiscate cash and other property without even charging business owners with a crime, let alone convicting them of one. Those powers limit economic freedom and opportunity in untold ways—with disparate impact on low-income populations—and slow the iterative growth individual entrepreneurs are otherwise working to achieve.

As these and other case studies included in this volume show, economic freedom must be at the center of any viable poverty-reduction strategy. What's more, to succeed, any strategy must be pursued within a culturally authentic context, which cannot be reliably achieved by well-meaning outsiders.

To summarize, Atlas Network invites consensus on the following principles as a solution to resolving "the outsider's dilemma:"

- Ensure outsiders are not substantively leading local change and recognize that governments, even domestic governments, often behave as outsiders when it comes to interfering with individual agency and choices.
- Support the vision of local, independent think tanks to achieve institutional change.
- Prioritize institutional increases in individual agency or economic freedom.

Building on that foundation, our challenge as outsiders is to discern the most promising projects to increase economic freedom around the world, those led by high performing think tanks, and to support those projects without interfering with the integrity of the local vision and strategy.

Our Approach

Just as the "positive deviant" approach helps to ensure success among low-income populations, it also informs Atlas Network's approach to facilitating innovation and success among a global network of independent think tanks. Like the Sternins, we create opportunities for our think tank partners to "cook" together as peers, which leads to new ideas and new levels of impact. In retrospect, those new ideas can seem serendipitous, and, in a sense, they are. But they are also the object of our facilitation strategy.

Our *Coach, Compete, Celebrate!* model for think tanks, which includes a mutually reinforcing suite of peer-based training, project grants, innovation awards, and networking programs, is designed to fuel and facilitate social change. We do it this way because it's what works best, it's the most proven method we have discovered so far to solve for "the outsider's dilemma." It's encouraging to see so many thoughtful scholars, practitioners, and experts of all stripes indirectly validating our strategy from a variety of disciplines.[16]

9

This new publication, *Poverty and Freedom,* is another example of our work to disseminate successful innovations for this cause. The selected case studies represent a snapshot of Atlas Network's global investments in think tank success. In each case, the vision for change emanates exclusively from the think tank leaders themselves. The goals are their own, the strategies are their own, and the innovations are their own. It's important to note that in no case do we represent a majority donor. Just like Miller, we only invest where serious initiative is already leading the way.

Our hands-off approach does not mean weak accountability. We observe high standards when it comes to the quality of the project plan and the clear articulation of the grantee's measurable outcomes. We do not prescribe vision or strategy changes to those plans, but we do provide training on impact measurement to provide accountability and to ensure prospective grantees are set up for success.[17]

You will see from the selection of projects in this volume a great diversity of topics, strategies, and goals. Despite this diversity, they all have in common an alignment with the three principles enumerated above. Namely, they reflect Atlas Network's limited role as outsider, they increase individual freedom, and they were led by a local vision for change.

We see those examples, plus the work of hundreds of other think tanks in our network, as central to our strategy for solving "the outsider's dilemma" in our quest to end poverty for good. It is a strategy that both aligns with classical liberal principles and is affirmed by the latest intellectual, multidisciplinary discoveries about wealth, poverty, and effective philanthropy.

We hope these case studies spark new ideas for achieving social change throughout the network, pave the way for new collaborations among think tanks and economic development experts, and inspire new levels of philanthropic support for this proven strategy to reduce poverty in the United States and around the world.

Notes

1. Ben Ramalingam, *Aid on the Edge of Chaos*, (Oxford: Oxford University Press, 2013), 207–10.

2. Note that for this volume the notion of ending poverty or reducing poverty refers to the achievement of sustained economic progress for populations of people and is distinct from and not to be conflated with the notion of temporary poverty relief.

3. Mauricio Miller, *The Alternative: Most of What You Think About Poverty Is Wrong,* (Lulu Publishing Services, 2017), 56.

4. Miller, *The Alternative*, 56.

5. Duncan Green, *How Change Happens*, (New York: Oxford University Press, 2016), 82.

6. For just one example, see http://ideas.time.com/2012/09/07/the-myth-of-bootstrapping/.

7. Richard Pascale, Jerry Sternin, and Monique Sternin, *The Power of Positive Deviance: How Unlikely Innovators Solve the World's Toughest Problems,* (Cambridge: Harvard University Press, 2010).

8. Duncan Green, *How Change Happens*, (Oxford: Oxford University Press, 2016), 25.

9. Eric Beinhocker, *The Origins of Wealth: The Radical Remaking of Economics,* (New York: Random House Business, 2007), 19, 318.

10. Beinhocker, *The Origins of Wealth,* 14.

11. See https://www.odi.org/sites/odi.org.uk/files/odi-assets/events-documents/5149.pdf.

12. See https://www.oecd.org/dac/effectiveness/parisdeclarationandaccraagendaforaction.htm.

13. Lydia Polgreen, "Home Improvement," *New York Times*, August 11, 2014, https://www.nytimes.com/2014/04/13/books/review/the-bright-continent-by-dayo-olopade.html.

14. Guy Lodge and Will Paxton, "Innovation in Think Tanks: Policy Influence and Change in Developing Countries," RSA, 2017.

15. Claudia R. Williamson and Rachel Mathers, "Economic Freedom, Culture, and Growth," Working Paper, Mercatus Center at George Mason University, 2009.

16. To provide just a few examples, see the work of Dan Honig, Nina Munk, Lant Pritchett, Michael Woolcock, and Pablo Yanguas.

17. Matt Warner, "Calling Your Shots: Measuring Think Tank Success," January 3, 2018, *https://www.atlasnetwork.org/news/article/calling-your-shots-in-2018-measuring-success-in-the-nonprofit-sector.*

Section I
The Outsider's Dilemma

One of the reasons the traditional aid model fails to achieve economic development is because it tends to substitute, to some fatal degree, outsider knowledge for local knowledge. If the premise of aid and philanthropy is to help poor places improve, outsiders must consider the ways their influence might do more harm than good. The broader aid community has long acknowledged the value of local knowledge and has taken many steps in good faith to incorporate local knowledge in aid planning. However, the power dynamics inherent in government-to-government or government-to-NGO aid-giving make it nearly impossible to avoid the imposition of outsider values and priorities on local communities.

This section explores the deeper reasons why local knowledge is important both at the systems level and at the level of individuals navigating their own paths to prosperity and reveals why local think tanks, rather than foreign and domestic governments, are well-positioned for donor partnership to resolve the dilemma outsiders face when trying to help. The articles in this section draw on a diverse set of important aid and economic development thinkers who wrestle with the issue of local knowledge, contributing useful insights for answering the question: As outsiders, what *can* we do to help?

Versions of the articles in this section are available at AtlasNetwork.org.

Overcoming the Outsider's Dilemma: Can Philanthropists Help the Developing World?

By Matt Warner

Executive Summary

Today's top-down economic development aid model is unavoidably flawed. The nature of economic development requires idiosyncratic solutions that can't be successfully designed or administered by outsiders. Instead, locally grown solutions aimed at transforming the institutional environment in favor of market growth, primarily through securing economic rights for the poor, represent the best chance for accelerating the pace of poverty alleviation throughout the world.

For outsiders, this represents a serious dilemma. Is there a way to help without interfering? A new strategy offered by Atlas Network successfully combines the resources of philanthropy with the local research and advocacy of independent, market-oriented think tanks working to strengthen the institutions that foster growth for the world's poor. Benchmarking their efforts to global indices like the Doing Business *report published by the World Bank, those think tanks are making measurable progress and the results are significant.*

Alex Georges co-founded ENERSA, a renewable energy company in Haiti, to help ease the transition from kerosene lamps to electricity. In the aftermath of the 2007 earthquake, solar power offered a quick and convenient way to provide power to mobile devices, relief workers, and those trying to rebuild their homes. His business was up and running, poised to meet the new demand. But a humanitarian-inspired dump of foreign solar panels flooded the local market, forcing layoffs at ENERSA and leaving Georges near bankruptcy.

Free stuff isn't always bad, especially in the immediate aftermath of a crisis. But for fragile economies, the unpredictable nature of humanitarian aid means it can reverse hard-won economic progress. What's more, in practice, there is little distinction between short-term emergency aid, which can be helpful, and long-term development programming, which is not. Today, they operate as a blurred permanent model that many experts claim is doing more harm than good. The good news is that there is now a better way, but it requires a completely new philanthropic strategy.

Aid Isn't Working

Oxford-trained economist Dambisa Moyo, who grew up in Zambia, writes in her book *Dead Aid: Why Aid is Not Working and How There Is a Better Way for Africa*, "Donors, development agencies, and policy-makers have, by and large, chosen to ignore the blatant alarm signals, and have continued to pursue the aid-based model even when it has become apparent that aid, under whatever guise, is not working." She reports that study after study demonstrate the failure of aid as a strategy for achieving real growth. While aid might deliver relief in a crisis, she concludes, "The idea that aid aimed at economic development helps to alleviate systemic poverty is a myth."

Simon Bland, head of Britain's department for international development in Kenya, told journalist Nina Munk, "I know that if you spend enough money on each person in a village, you will change their lives. . . . The problem is, when you walk away, what happens?" Bland has witnessed the precarious state of aid-dependent communities. Not only does aid contribute to the problems of instability: aid delays and distorts the path for the kind of sustainable development those communities need for long-term growth and independence.

Munk, a contributing editor at *Vanity Fair* magazine, spent six years shadowing Jeffrey Sachs, perhaps the most famous development expert in favor of more aid. Munk started the project thinking that her reporting might help raise awareness about Sachs' $120 million Millennium Villages Project, an all-of-the-above strategy designed to help poor villages make the great leap forward to economic development. In the end, she published an unflattering appraisal titled, "The Idealist: Jeffrey Sachs and the Quest to End Poverty," which details how his approach is having a devastating effect on economic development.

She writes, "Jeffrey Sachs' observations on the ground were necessarily limited—by the pressures of time, by language, culture, education, background, preconceptions and ingrained models of thought." She adds, "In effect, [Sachs] wanted us to trust him, to accept without question his approach to ending poverty, to participate in a kind of collective magical thinking."

She observed first hand the costs of that "magical thinking," in this case the belief that an outsider with limited knowledge can solve other people's economic problems for them. The result is example after example of major investments in new crops that found no customers, new trade centers that found no traders, and new jobs that could not be sustained. Even when efforts had positive outcomes, they could not continue without further aid, a result completely at odds with the purpose and pitch behind Sachs' development strategy.

Most practitioners are well aware of these problems and for more than a decade have tried to overcome them through better program design. Those efforts have underscored the need to do development differently, but because they fail to fully account for the undermining influence of the outsider, they fall short of achieving lasting prosperity for those in need.

Institutions Matter

When it comes to achieving prosperity, we have learned that institutions such as property rights, the rule of law, and free markets are paramount. For decades, international organizations and governments have pushed some version of those kinds of consensus reforms from the top down as conditions for trade, aid, and credit—often with tragic results.

17

We've learned the hard way that property rights systems are unlikely to "stick" if imported. Instead, they have to be developed from within, locally grown, both to ensure buy-in and—more importantly—as a means to discover the unique cultural mechanisms necessary for informal norms to transition smoothly to well-functioning formal systems.

In South Africa, as noted earlier, land titling increased for post-Apartheid government housing tenants only after the Free Market Foundation, a local nongovernmental organization that champions property rights for the poor, led a community reform effort that relied on voluntary participation. This approach succeeded in strengthening the institution of property rights because it was driven primarily by the individual decisions of its beneficiaries.

In their book *Why Nations Fail*, authors Daron Acemoglu and James Robinson point to the importance of getting institutions right but at the same time offer the crucial insight that "No two societies create the same institutions." Successful institutions might hold many things in common, but their design—and the process for achieving that design—is necessarily idiosyncratic and very likely to fail if planned by an outside mind or organization.

Foreign Governments: The Ultimate Outsiders

Consider this uncomfortable truth: while there might be differences in motivation and intention, today's intellectual hubris about economic development follows closely on the heels of a long and disturbing history of paternalism between the world's rich countries and those less developed. The prevailing philosophy of aid has its roots in a colonial past. In their book, Acemoglu and Robinson describe that past in all its brutality and pin some of the blame for the state of today's most dysfunctional governments on that legacy. Even then, early motivations had the veneer of helping. Biographer Adam Hochschild explained how the monstrous Belgian King Leopold II, who infamously ruled over the Congo in the late 19th century with almost complete disregard for human suffering, enlisted the world's best explorers by describing the mission in only altruistic terms, promising to abolish the slave trade and, as a means to improve their legal institutions, "procuring them just and impartial arbitration."

This legacy shows up in the bias held today in favor of technical expertise and centrally planned solutions. It blinds the outsider to the faulty premise that one can and should solve economic problems on behalf of the poor.

In his latest book, *The Tyranny of Experts: Economists, Dictators, and the Forgotten Rights of the Poor*, William Easterly, professor of economics at New York University and co-director of its Development Research Institute, traces the historical progression of state-led, authoritarian bias inherent in international economic development and warns that "the exhortation that all development discussions must lead . . . to a recommended philanthropic action inhibits clear thinking."

It's an important point because the stakes are high. Economist Chris Coyne is the author of *Doing Bad by Doing Good: Why Humanitarian Action Fails*. He observes, "[H]umanitarian action has over time become increasingly intertwined with the broader military and foreign policy objectives of governments," making the dilemma that much more intractable for well-intentioned philanthropists in the economic development space.

Coyne's research confirms the problems created by the outsider's hubris. He painstakingly demonstrates how the dominant and rapidly expanding state-led approach "neglects or downplays the complex economic, legal, and political systems underpinning the effectiveness of designed organizations and institutions." The unfortunate result is not just failed economic development but a geopolitical system even more vulnerable to conflict of interest and corruption.

Like Easterly, Coyne doesn't offer much of a philanthropic alternative, but in his concluding chapter, he writes, "[F]ocusing on ways to . . . remov[e] barriers to economic freedom will yield benefits significantly greater than those from the best spent foreign assistance." This observation echoes Easterly's emphasis on restoring economic rights for the poor, but as outsiders, it still leaves us in the same dilemma. How can we help the world's poor if the intervention itself is part of the problem?

The outsider's dilemma is woefully underappreciated, even ignored. Foreign governments continue to spend large sums on development projects. Ignoring the dilemma instead of confronting it head-on is distracting us from finding a solution and, instead, leading us into strange territory, indeed.

Short-Term versus Long-Term Solutions

Consider that in 2017, one of the most prominent debates in economic development pitted Bill Gates against development expert Chris Blattman on whether to give poor people chickens or cash. Both cases are no doubt borne of noble motives, but neither is a proven method for achieving prosperity, and both completely sidestep what has proven to be the most consequential problem: the institutions governing where poor people live.

Research shows when poor people relocate to countries with economic rights for the poor, they thrive. As Harvard development expert Lant Pritchett explains it, "There are no poor people. There are people living in poor places." Giving someone a chicken or a tidy sum of cash will do little in a country that makes it nearly impossible for them to be productive because there are too many barriers to enterprise and too few legally secured economic rights.

If we don't figure out a way to remove barriers to the free exercise of economic rights, every other approach will fail. As 2015 Nobel Prize–winner Angus Deaton explains in *The Great Escape: Health, Wealth, and the Origins of Inequality*, "When the conditions for development are present, aid is not required. When local conditions are hostile to development, aid is not useful, and it will do harm if it perpetuates those conditions."

Of course, we should exercise great care before dismissing as insignificant what a modest cash gift or a chicken might do for an individual or a family. At the same time, though, we must also focus on the larger problem that, if solved, could have much more far-reaching impact. Coyne cites political theorist and moral philosopher Michael Walzer, who writes, "It is, of course, immediately necessary to feed the hungry, to stop the killing. Relief comes before repair, but repair, despite the risks it brings with it, should always be the long-term goal—so that crises do not become "recurrent and routine." You can accept that challenge while preserving a healthy respect for the outsider's dilemma, but taken together, they require a radically different approach to helping the world's poor. As it turns out, such an approach is emerging already.

A New Strategy for Outsiders

Atlas Network serves more than 480 independent think tanks in 96 countries. Each advocates their own unique reform agenda based on the principles of the free society and the economic rights necessary for all people to achieve financial well-being.

Those organizations represent the missing link between the need to remove barriers to the free exercise of economic rights, on the one hand, and the necessity of cultivating locally grown solutions to bridge today's informal norms with tomorrow's strong institutions, on the other.

They represent a philanthropic opportunity for outsiders to pursue a new strategy for ending poverty, one that overcomes the outsider's dilemma, while building on the wisdom and warnings of a diverse set of experts.

Small Reforms, Big Impact

Entrepreneurship and economic development experts William Baumol, Carl Schramm, and Robert Litan emphasize in their book *Good Capitalism, Bad Capitalism* the importance of economic freedom in achieving growth, particularly in countries with high levels of poverty. Recognizing the political realities many countries face, they concluded that significant results could be gained even from achieving reform "policies *at the margin* (emphasis in the original)."

How do we identify such marginal policies? In essence, by their association with affirmative answers to the following four questions:

1. Is it easy to start, grow, and close a business?
2. Is it easy to realize the rewards of productive behavior (i.e., the rule of law, freedom of contract, property rights, simple taxes)?
3. Is it hard to realize the rewards of unproductive behavior (fraud, theft, rent-seeking)?
4. Is it hard to stop competitors, except by competing (i.e., barriers to trade and investment)?

Those are the kind of policies measured by, for example, *Economic Freedom of the World* report and the *Doing Business* report. Of those policy changes, Baumol et al. later write, "These are no small matters." They continue, "Taking some or all of these steps can quickly lead to results." In fact, they cite the *Doing Business* report where it "documents sharp jumps in the numbers of businesses registered and increases in business investments in countries that have streamlined their business registration systems."

Doing Development Differently

A new strategy for economic development first recognizes that outsiders cannot effectively design local solutions. Local independent think tanks with the knowledge, capacity, and ambition to remove barriers to economic freedom and restore economic rights are the best qualified to do that.

The new strategy also recognizes that the most practical way forward in many countries is simply to chip away at those barriers to economic freedom that prevent entrepreneurs and everyday people from being productive, and such reforms are significant. At the conclusion of his latest book, Easterly clarifies that he is hopeful about the future because even "an incremental positive change in freedom will yield a positive change in well-being for the world's poor."

Moreover, the new strategy recognizes there is a role for outsiders. Philanthropists can fuel local research and advocacy projects around the world. They can fund independent organizations that are committed to the reforms that build and strengthen the institutions necessary for economic development. With current resources, think tanks around the world are consistently achieving significant reforms, and each of those reforms has a measurable impact on key indices and positive and measurable benefits for the poor.

With more help, they can achieve even more.

Today's aid programs will never achieve the big results we truly desire—the end of poverty worldwide. Our best chance at nearing this goal is to advance a strategy that recognizes, at its core, the crucial knowledge and leadership that only local people can provide for their own exodus from poverty.

Unleashing Productive Knowledge: Aid Reformers Confront the Outsider's Dilemma

By Matt Warner

Executive Summary

There is growing consensus from experts and practitioners that international aid needs dramatic change in order to become more effective, more transparent, and less vulnerable to criticisms of waste, corruption, and even net harm.

A new school of thought from the emerging discipline of complexity research supports a major rethinking of aid and the relationship between "outsiders" and the communities they hope to help. Despite this, reform momentum seems to remain concentrated around improving—as opposed to challenging the role of—aid agencies and the government bureaucracies throughout the developing world with whom they partner.

An alternative interpretation of complexity research suggests minimizing the economic role of aid agencies and governments in developing nations and maximizing economic freedom for individuals to steer development toward a more reliable path to prosperity.

Introduction

The top-down, foreign-led design of international aid programs has been long criticized for its overreliance on simplistic, linear strategies at odds with the complex way nations develop.

Beginning with Nobel Prize development economist P. T. Bauer's heretical 1971 book, *Dissent on Development*, a long list of intellectual heavyweights and experts have rigorously challenged the aid industry's juggernaut-like way of trying to help the world's poor.

Nobel Prize economist Eleanor Ostrom dismissed the contribution of aid agencies, complaining that they may at times say the right things but lack a deep understanding of the problem.

Even more damning, Richard Dowden, director of the Africa Institute, once suggested that modern aid agencies can be even less thoughtful about local people and cultures than were their colonial forbearers. What's more, Angus Deaton, whose Nobel Prize was awarded in 2015, concluded in his 2013 book *The Great Escape: Health, Wealth, and the Origins of Inequality* that aid agencies might be doing more harm than good in the communities they are meant to serve.

Encouragingly, several of today's mainstream academics and even some aid practitioners sympathize with those criticisms and advocate energetically for reform. Their proposed solutions, however, might not go far enough in demonstrating they have learned the lessons of aid's failures. Instead, what appears to be an unshakable commitment to the central roles of aid agencies and national governments in steering development might represent just another version of the same fatal conceit that plagued the predecessors of today's aid advocates. If that's true, the question is how might we better use their insights to further our common goal of seeing the world's poor prosper?

Confronting the Inefficacy of Aid So Far

Beginning in 2003, the Organisation for Economic Co-operation and Development (OECD) has spearheaded a global effort to improve the effectiveness of aid, specifically addressing aid's historic paternalism, lack of transparency, and failure to demonstrate significant results. To date, more than 160 countries representing both donors and recipients have signed on to this effort and have agreed to a new set of principles that continue to be refined. The most recent version follows the four themes below:

1. Ownership of development priorities by developing countries: Partnerships for development can only succeed if they are led by developing countries, implementing approaches that are tailored to country-specific situations and needs.

25

2. Focus on results: Our investments and efforts must have a lasting effect on eradicating poverty and reducing inequality, on sustainable development, and on enhancing developing countries' capacities, aligned with the priorities and policies set out by developing countries.

3. Inclusive development partnerships: Openness, trust, mutual respect, and learning are at the core of effective partnerships in support of development goals, recognizing the different and complementary goals of all actors.

4. Transparency and accountability to each other: Mutual accountability and accountability to the intended beneficiaries of our cooperation, as well as to our respective citizens, organizations, constituents, and shareholders, is critical to delivering results. Transparent practices form the basis for enhanced accountability.

The observance of those principles is meant to subdue the influence of donor countries to make more room for recipient countries' own knowledge about their specific and complex needs. The hope has been to start doing things better, to learn from past mistakes, and to introduce better listening and better measurement to focus on results.

Unfortunately, the pace of change has been disappointing. The 2016 report of The Global Partnership for Effective Development Co-operation, the organization tasked with monitoring progress on the OECD goals, offers mixed results and little cause for celebration. Despite its upbeat tone, the report underscores the persistent, and perhaps inevitable, challenges associated with outsiders trying to help without interfering. As just one example, progress toward the elimination of perverse practices such as conditional support (strings attached to aid that serve donor country interests even though they might undermine local priorities) remains well below targets.

While the principles set forth by the OECD do speak to important insights about the type of solution needed, some experts are starting to question whether we fully understand the complexity of the problem itself.

Aid and Dynamism

One of the more helpful ways to think about why traditional aid has not worked in developing economies is explained in Ben Ramalingam's 2013 book, *Aid on the Edge of Chaos: Rethinking International Cooperation in a Complex World*. He compares international aid's approach to the misguided forest fire prevention policies that dominated late 19th-century national parks. He explains, "[f]ire policies have not protected the forests but in fact have placed them at considerably greater risk," in part because the intervention to prevent fires itself disrupts the natural process of emergent forest health. The counterintuitive warning then is, "preventing small fires can lead to large fires."

Like ecological systems, economies are also complex in the technical sense, meaning a linear strategy employed to influence economic outcomes will fail to account for the near countless factors that threaten the outcomes such plans seek.

Those factors are not only exceedingly numerous, they are interdependent, so how they affect each other cannot be reliably predicted using traditional methods that tend to isolate variables for testing and prediction. As a result, interventions driven by linear strategies, even those supported by evidence, run afoul of functioning complex systems.

Complexity Science

This confounding dynamism has inspired a new line of research under the broad banner of complexity science with an aim, in part, to discover how we can do development better. In one sense, this approach is a nod to Friedrich von Hayek's 1974 Nobel Prize lecture, "The Pretense of Knowledge," in which he calls on the scientific community to recognize its own limits in applying known scientific tools to complex problems. And yet, it's also an attempt to transcend those limits by improving the scientific toolbox that experts employ in the face of that complexity.

This tension is nothing new to scientific thinkers. In the 2015 *New York Times* best-selling book *Super Forecasting: The Art and Science of Prediction*, authors Philip E. Tetlock and Dan Gardner write, "For centuries, scientists had supposed that growing knowledge must lead to greater predictability because reality was like a clock—an awesomely big and complicated clock but still a clock—and the more scientists learned about its innards, how the gears grind together, how the weights and springs function, the better they could capture its operations with deterministic equations and predict what it would do."

Tetlock and Gardner explain how the work of meteorologist Edward Lorenz showed, as early as the 1970s, that "in nonlinear systems like the atmosphere, even small changes [or errors] in initial conditions can mushroom to enormous proportions." For economic development, this means underpowered and simplistic strategies are more likely to lead to ruin than they are prosperity. To replace the clock comparison, Tetlock and Gardner offer the concept of a cloud as a more fitting representation of complex reality. While a lot might be known about clouds, we're unable, for example, to predict the shape of one.

They conclude, "Unpredictability and predictability coexist uneasily in the intricately interlocking systems that make up our bodies, our societies, and the cosmos. How predictable something is depends on what we are trying to predict, how far into the future, and under what circumstances." That line between unpredictability and predictability echoes the "edge of chaos" that Ramalingam suggests is the sandbox we must play in if we want to get better at economic development.

In practice, this means recognizing that complex systems analysis must eschew the search for a single solution, what Ramalingam calls "best practicitis." He calls on aid agencies to first cure themselves of this ailment and, secondly, to adopt a new mindset that looks instead for self-organized, emergent solutions within specific contexts. Those solutions, when identified, cannot simply be bottled for redistribution. Instead, aid practitioners must seek ways to accelerate the iterative nature of innovation diffusion among networks to spread the solution's impact.

The knowledge relevant for finding the solution in a complex system is what anomalous outliers operating within the system discover, as evidenced by the outcomes they exhibit, combined with the knowledge others possess within the system that allows them to recognize, value, and adopt the innovation for themselves. To be clear, outside knowledge, as observed and selectively absorbed by those within the system, is also important. Indeed, global exchange of goods, services, and ideas has been one of the most important accelerants of human flourishing. The key difference is *who* is in charge of adopting and applying those ideas to the benefit of individuals? Outsiders or the individuals themselves?

Productive Knowledge in Complex Systems

Economist Ricardo Hausmann and his co-authors in *The Atlas of Economic Complexity: Mapping Paths to Prosperity* refer to this knowledge as productive knowledge. This is the knowledge that is critical for a solution to emerge in a complex system, and for Hausmann, it is the knowledge that produces saleable economic activity. This knowledge is distributed widely across individuals and discovered only through the dynamic process of those individuals engaging one another in various contexts, such as in a market, making decisions on their own behalf.

Of course, the word "distributed" is misleading since it implies some act is undertaken by some actor to do the distributing. In fact, the critical knowledge already exists within the individuals themselves as a result of their various experiences and cognition. Furthermore, much of that knowledge is tacit, meaning those who possess it might not even be conscious of it, might not be able to articulate it, nor would they necessarily recognize its influence on how they evaluate options in any decision set they face. Lastly, and importantly, productive knowledge cannot be obtained by outsiders to exercise on others' behalf.

Unlike Ramalingam, who seeks to reform aid agencies so they can better manage complexity, Hausmann places his hopes for reform on countries' ability to achieve product differentiation. He writes, "The policy message for most countries is clear: create an environment where a greater diversity of productive activities can thrive, paying particular attention to activities that are relatively more complex or that open up more opportunities."

Using international trade data, Hausmann and his co-authors created what they call the Economic Complexity Index to measure, by proxy, the productive knowledge of a country by assessing the complexity of the products it exports relative to other countries. They claim that economic complexity drives long-run levels of income and growth. To provide some guidance on what to do with that insight, they also developed the Complexity Outlook Index, which measures the potential set of products a country could be making, weighted by their complexity, and based on their own productive capabilities. Taken together, Hausmann et al. claim their measures predict future growth better than virtually any other variables tested in the growth literature.

While Hausmann et al. prescribe no role for aid agencies, per se, in using their tools, they do intend for their indices to be used widely by anyone invested in economic development, including firms looking to relocate or diversify. Despite that broad invitation, most of their suggestions for action lie within the purview of national governments, and one hopes the biggest impact of their work won't be the expansion of industrial policy throughout the developing world.

The last thing developing countries need their governments to do is to try to pick winners and losers in the marketplace. Development economist William Easterly's research on international trade has revealed the "power law" of export success, which observes that for some phenomena, large outcomes are more likely than would be suggested by normal distributions. As a result, the chance of picking a winner actually goes down exponentially the higher the threshold used to define success. For developing countries especially, this means the stakes for such a gamble are too high.

Improving Governments to Improve Aid

In 2017, Harvard University's Matt Andrews, Lant Pritchett, and Michael J. V. Woolcock published *Building State Capability: Evidence, Analysis, Action*, which presents both an argument for focusing on OECD's second principle, capacity development, as the linchpin of success in economic development, as well as sets forth an improvement guide for government bureaucracies.

The authors argue that until governments in developing countries are more sophisticated and competent, they never will be able to deliver the kind of public services aid programs are meant to support. For them, this is the key to economic development. A central and persuasive tenet of their prescribed strategy is recognizing that institutions cannot simply be transplanted from foreign countries, a practice they call isomorphic mimicry. Because they are part of complex systems, institutions have to be developed locally, in context, so that they represent the needs, culture, and practices of local environments.

To help governments improve their capacity, then, the authors have developed a program for bureaucrats called "Problem-Driven Iterative Adaptation" (PDIA). Rooted in the insights of complexity science, PDIA offers a series of exercises for government teams to work through to discover their own unique pathways to bureaucratic competence. The steps in the process are worth repeating here since they echo the broader traits of complex systems solutions:

- Focus on specific problems in a particular local context as nominated and prioritized by local actors.
- Identify motivational problems.
- Foster active, ongoing experimental iterations with new ideas, gathering lessons from these iterations to allow solutions to emerge.
- Establish an authorizing environment for decision-making that encourages experimentation and positive deviance.
- Engage broad sets of agents with highly varied skill sets to ensure that reforms are viable, legitimate, and relevant.

Notably, each of those points can be restated in a way that illuminates core principles of the market economy, which is the complex system at the heart of successful economic development. For example, "prioritization by local actors" recognizes the value of what Hayek called the "knowledge of time and place." It is the knowledge that individuals possess about their own preferences and circumstances that cannot be centralized or obtained for productive use by others, and it echoes the productive knowledge of Hausmann.

Recognizing the importance of motivational problems mirrors the central insight of economics that incentives matter, particularly given the principal-agent problem many aid workers must try to navigate. In its broadest context, this problem refers to the complications that arise when someone is meant to act on someone else's behalf, which is why outsiders in the context of aid are at a particular disadvantage.

"Iterative change" implies an unpredictable but productive evolution of change that learns along the way. That learning and change may implicate disruption of old models to get to a new solution. This concept is not unlike Joseph Schumpeter's description of entrepreneurial change via creative destruction, the unpredictable but likely consequence of a complex system unfettered by centralized attempts to impose linear-based outcomes.

A key motivation for emphasizing the importance of the authorizing environment for decision-making in *Building State Capability* is the insight that decentralized decision-making is a necessary approach to achieving innovative solutions. Similar to the productive efficiency of markets that are rooted in decentralized rights to property, decisions are best made by those who bear the costs and, at the same time, stand to reap the benefits of those decisions. In this way, all decisions implicate tradeoffs. Central authorities cannot grasp all relevant tradeoffs in a complex system such as a developing economy.

Lastly, recognizing that complex problems are best tackled by a diversity of people calls to mind the powerful influence of specialization in achieving exponential gains. Furthermore, what determines whether something has achieved vibrancy, legitimacy, and relevance in a complex system is that broad set of third parties whose individual decisions and actions either support or fail to support the success of any initiative or product. This type of consumer sovereignty does not imply an all-knowing or perfectly rational set of third parties. It simply means success is dependent on the actions of many independent actors and the special contributions they make that, when aggregated, support a growing economy.

It's encouraging to see mainstream experts conclude that the answer to economic development has to do with those core economic ideas. It seems unlikely, however, that local governments, following a foreign how-to guide on discovering emergent solutions for their own bureaucracies, will be an effective solution to the problem of underdevelopment. In fact, based on their own measures of state capability, the authors put the odds of success dismally low for most developing countries, with only eight on track to achieve their definition of strong capability this century.

Despite their intellectual contributions, the framework these thought leaders operate within is too limited. It takes for granted that the solution to economic development will emanate from the technical knowledge of foreigners, and that the solution will be worked out between those foreigners and the local governments attempting to run the countries where development is needed most. Short of that grander ambition, however, their analysis of public policy may leave a clue for how best to apply the insights of complexity science to unlock the productive knowledge Hausmann writes about.

Public Policy and State Capability

In looking at a state's capability to advance various public policies, Andrews et al. distinguish among the simple and the complex using four categories that represent the difficulty a bureaucracy would have implementing and maintaining them:

- Is the policy transaction intensive?
- Does it require a lot of discretionary decisions be made?
- Does it serve the public or impose an obligation on them?
- Is it dependent on known or unknown technology?

Is your activity. . .	Does producing successful outcomes from your activity. . .
Transaction intensive?	Require many agents to act or few
Locally discretionary?	Require that the implementing agents make finely based distinctions about the "state of the world"? Are these distinctions difficult for a third part to assess?
Service or imposition of obligation	Do the people in direct contact with your agents want or not want the agent to succeed?
Based on a known technology	Is there an accepted handbook or body of knowledge for doing what you are trying to do or will this require innovation (not just context)

Re-creation of Figure 5.1: Four key analytic questions about an activity to classify the capability needed, found on page 108 of *Building State Capability*, (Oxford: Oxford University Press, 2017).

The authors' goal in *Building State Capability* is to help national and local governments around the world become better at carrying out the more complex policies, namely, those that are transaction intensive; require bureaucratic agents to make wise, discretionary decisions; impose unpleasant or unwanted obligations on the public; and depend on the bureaucracy innovating successfully.

Undoubtedly, they see the daunting nature of their chosen task. They concede, therefore, that there ought to be a "genuine debate about the tasks a government can realistically perform," especially when other civil society actors, including private organizations, can perform those functions just as well or better. This observation begins to look like a case for limited government, but they also suggest there should be a plan to reintegrate those functions back into government in the future as state capability improves.

This begs the question, though: in a world of struggling state capability, why not begin instead by emphasizing proven public policies that rely less on government for success? That means advocating for those policies that are less transaction intensive, less dependent on omniscient government agents, and less burdensome on citizens: in short, those policies that depend only on basic competencies that are clearly understood by those charged with carrying them out.

It seems those are the types of policies that would go the furthest in demonstrating appreciation for the insights of complexity science; namely, that the most productive knowledge critical to discovering solutions is possessed by the individuals themselves who are the ostensible beneficiaries of aid programming. The conclusion, then, must be to expand the decision set for individuals as much as possible to provide maximum flexibility for discovering productive change and growth.

Public Policy and Economic Freedom

Nobel laureate Amartya Sen's 1999 book *Development as Freedom* details the nonseverable relationship between those two ideas. He writes, "The perspective of freedom has been used both in the evaluative analysis for assessing change and in the descriptive and predictive analysis in seeing freedom as a causally effective factor in generating rapid change."

It is precisely the freedom within complex systems that allows solutions to emerge. If governments and aid agencies are to have a positive influence on economic development, they must be judged within the context of freedom. Sen explains, "A variety of social institutions relating to the operation of markets, administrations, legislatures, political parties, nongovernmental organizations, the judiciary, the media, and the community, in general, contribute to the process of development precisely through their effects on enhancing and sustaining individual freedoms."

There is an abundance of those types of policies to choose from in places such as the Fraser Institute's *Economic Freedom of the World* report or the World Bank's *Doing Business* report, both of which assess countries based on their policies defining individual economic choice and government's scope and functions.

Both reports showcase the impact of policies that make it easier and cheaper to start a business, easier and cheaper to trade across borders, and easier and cheaper to register property and get construction permits. Consequently, both reports make the case for relatively smaller governments charged with fewer unnecessary regulations to enforce.

Admittedly, many good policies, even some of those included in those global indices, require strong institutions supported by competent and capable governments. How much more likely, though, are governments to do those things well if they, as Andrews et al. suggest we debate, are limited in their tasks to only those that are truly necessary?

Yet, in the same way that outsiders blunder when they try to help other people achieve economic success, they also blunder when they try to get other governments to strengthen their institutions. In an article published in the *American Journal of Economics and Sociology*, economists Peter Boettke, Christopher Coyne, and Peter Leeson use the term "sticky" to describe how successfully institutions persist within a country. In their analysis of what makes stickiness more likely, they conclude that chances are best when local actors lead the process of improvement.

For this reason, think tanks that are focused on expanding economic choices for all stand the best chance of leading effective change. It is their civic entrepreneurship that determines what reforms are needed, which of them are possible, and what form they should take to achieve relevance and sustainability in the local context.

Unleashing Productive Knowledge in a Complex System

Improvements in scores in the *Economic Freedom of the World* report and *Doing Business* report can mean more and more people lifting themselves out of poverty. For example, the Centre for Civil Society in India succeeded in convincing the Modi government to eliminate minimum capital requirements for new businesses, a policy that disproportionately burdens the poor and one that scores high on Andrews et al.'s complexity spectrum for bureaucratic capacity. Its elimination then is a win-win for economic development.

Changes like this align with the insight from complexity science that the knowledge needed for economic development is possessed by those in poverty since they are in the best position to assess whether they have enough capital to take on the risk of starting a business. It certainly makes more sense than concluding the best way forward is to make aid agencies more adaptive, or bureaucracies more capable, or national governments more calculating in picking winners and losers in the product marketplace. Those actions do nothing to expand economic choices for the true drivers of poverty reduction: the poor themselves.

As outsiders, we can play our part by supporting independent research and advocacy think tanks led by local intellectual leaders who recognize that the future economic success of their country is a function of the expanded economic opportunities all people enjoy as their governments attempt less economic planning on their behalf. This solution shares in the spirit of the OECD principles in seeking solutions at the local level and takes them to their natural conclusion.

The teams associated with Andrews, Ramalingam, and Hausmann have made major contributions to our understanding of complexity, and yet most of their hopes for using that increased knowledge are pinned on the centralized decision-making capabilities of aid agencies and national governments. Their solutions do take seriously the insight that within complex systems, individuals freed to engage in dynamic processes will discover solutions that are more promising than their centralized, top-down counterparts. Yet they underappreciate the big opportunity this insight represents. It's an opportunity to transform the way we think about helping others around the world by first recognizing that because productive knowledge is widely distributed in a developing economy, our first priority is to ensure we are not interfering with or obstructing the productive use of that knowledge.

Hausmann says it well when he writes, "The secret to modernity is that we collectively use large volumes of knowledge, while each one of us holds only a few bits of it." The key then is to stop trying to centralize that knowledge via outsiders or governments and to simply unleash it. The more we resist the temptation to solve economic problems for others, the more we will improve on that score. Ramalingam offers us this final piece of encouragement, "Even if a narrow, simplistic, mechanistic, reductionist form of global altruism is our legacy, it needn't be our fate."

SECTION II
Think Tank Impact and Measurement

In light of "the outsider's dilemma," local think tanks represent an "undervalued" opportunity to support local leadership in achieving social change. What's more, over the last two decades, local think tanks have grown both in number and sophistication. For example, today there are more than 480 think tanks representing 95 countries in Atlas Network's directory of independent partners. Those organizations offer unique visions for local change based on local knowledge and local priorities. How to determine who and what is worth supporting can be a major undertaking.

In philanthropy, many struggle with important topics like impact and measurement. This is also an area where outsider influence, in the well-meaning pursuit of accountability, can distort viable pathways for success. Reconciliation is achievable, however. There are proven ways donors can be judicious about their giving, hold grantees to high standards of accountability, and at the same time avoid interfering in local visions and strategies for change. This section introduces some of the key concepts and supporting research that inform Atlas Network's grant-making practice. This section also details some of the theory behind Atlas Network's strategy for facilitating innovation and ambition across the network of current and potential grantees.

Versions of the articles in this section are available at AtlasNetwork.org.

Calling Your Shots: Measuring Think Tank Success

By Matt Warner

I grew up playing pool with my Dad. We played "no slop," which means you had to call your shot before you struck the cue ball. If you sunk your ball in a way you didn't intend, you would have to pull it out, put it back on the table, and lose your turn.

The power of this principle is further demonstrated in the way we celebrate the lore of people like Babe Ruth. The story goes that in one game, the Sultan of Swat famously pointed past the outfield to announce his intention to swing for the fences. And, of course, when he hit a home run just as he signaled he would, it gave great credibility to his skill as a hitter.

Willingness to invite accountability by publicly announcing one's intentions to achieve a specific result is fast becoming an important practice for the successful nonprofit leader.

In the fall of 2016, Libertad y Progreso (LyP), a nonprofit think tank in Buenos Aires, Argentina, announced plans to raise awareness about the injustice of a tariff on certain technologies like laptops and tablets. The LyP team shared their plans with us at Atlas Network and explained why they believed their efforts would lead to the tariff's repeal. "Calling their shot" in this way made it clear to us that if we supported their work with a grant, we would know without ambiguity whether or not the investment paid off—and, given the relatively short timeline LyP had suggested, we knew we could be confident in assigning much of the credit to them.

By summer 2017, after a rigorous research and advocacy campaign that communicated robust findings with a simple yet powerful message, the tariff was repealed in Argentina. I am confident

LyP's work achieved the impact it intended, and I attribute that confidence to the way in which its leaders were willing to hold themselves publicly accountable to a very clear outcome.

The "calling your shot" principle does much more than just increase your credibility with key audiences. When fully embraced, it ends up permeating everything an organization does and how it decides to do it. Once a specific outcome has been targeted by the team and announced, downstream activity becomes more focused and disciplined as that which needs to be done becomes clear.

Debates over tactics, for example, become much less vulnerable to misguided conclusions based on what is familiar, popular, or safe. It becomes harder to fall into the old trap of what one Harvard team calls "isomorphic mimicry," which is the practice of pursuing success by copying what you can replicate from successful peers. The reason this can be a mistake, in my observation, is it confuses what success actually is. Instead of discovering how to *be* a successful organization, the goal becomes *appearing to be* a successful organization, a difference that at times may be subtle but is, in fact, of great consequence.

At a workshop I attended in Boston, nonprofit guru Dan Pallotta told a story about his early days working to create highly successful fundraising events for AIDS research. After some surprising wins right out of the gate, Pallotta decided he needed to keep the momentum going by announcing a list of new cities and dates for upcoming events. His team was appalled. 'We don't have any events set up in those cities," they said. He replied something to the effect of, 'Well, we'd better!' And, of course, they scrambled and made it happen.

I'm not suggesting nonprofit leaders make a habit of shooting from the hip like that. But this story does make an important point about the kind of leaders we want to be. Are we willing to hold ourselves accountable to a public goal? Are we willing to be ambitious even when we don't know exactly how we're going to achieve success?

What if we fall short? Of course it's possible. But I believe if we aim high and fall short, we will have achieved more than we would have otherwise. And if we are sincerely determined and committed to succeed, our failures will give us a better vision of what we need to do differently, thus setting us on an even stronger course for success. I've also seen that as long as we remain transparent about our progress and make sure we are communicating our commitment to new plans in response to failure, those who have supported us will keep the faith.

Having the courage to "call your shot" is important. In the nonprofit sector, we suffer from something so central we're reminded of it every time we mention our sector's name. Without profit, we have no natural margin to measure success. We have no margin that makes innovation or failure the only two options. Instead, we have to create our own margins for innovation. By reaching just beyond what we already comfortably know how to do and then holding ourselves publicly accountable to a specific set of outcomes, we create a margin for innovation and success that will then clarify our path forward and, just as importantly, help us see what we no longer have the luxury of maintaining.

As a service organization to other nonprofits, Atlas Network always wants to practice what we preach. What shots are we calling? For one, we want to contribute to 1,000,000 people around the globe lifting themselves out of poverty.

We're calling that shot. Is it ambitious? Yes.

Do we know exactly how to do it? No. But we have a plan.

We have learned an incredible amount over the last two years about how to approach this goal. We have built a robust and highly selective grant-making process that awards $5 million per year to the most promising projects in our nonprofit sector, those that call their shot by enumerating specific outcomes. A subset of those grants go to projects, like the tariff repeal in Argentina, that seek to expand economic choices for every day people.

Each year, we plan to do more. Please hold us accountable. We don't know with certainty that we will succeed, but, like Babe Ruth, we have the confidence to believe we can do it. And we're organizing ourselves in every way possible to pull it off.

If you're a nonprofit leader working for big wins this year, we want to know what shots you're calling so we can cheer you on as we all swing for the fences in pursuit of global prosperity.

Choosing a Bigger Pond: Why Think Tank Leaders Need a Global Network

By Matt Warner

Executive Summary

Without profit motive, can nonprofit leaders be as innovative and successful as their profit-seeking counterparts? As it turns out, there's a type of motivation that transcends the drive for profit, and it can influence the behavior of nonprofit leaders toward improving results as well. It's called social comparison—and research shows it can be even more powerful than money.

The first time my wife and I visited Great Falls, a national park on the Potomac River just north of Washington, D.C., we knew nothing about it. We pulled up to the Maryland side of the river and started walking toward a sign labeled "Falls" pointing into the woods.

After about 100 yards, we came upon a beautiful series of cascading falls that passed under the footbridge where we stood. The water was rushing fast and loud. Growing up in Florida where the flat elevation makes for few waterfalls, we were both impressed.

After taking a few pictures, one of us wondered aloud where the trail led to next. People were coming and going in both directions, so we decided to continue down the path. Less than a minute later we heard it. The dull roar of what turned out to be an incredible expanse of water churning. The full scope of it soon came into view.

These were the falls that were actually "great." We were completely stunned, in total awe of the scale. We were amused at our own ignorance in thinking that what we had visited just minutes earlier, easily 1/100th the size of what was now before us, was the main attraction.

What determines whether falls are great? Why were we initially satisfied with the much smaller falls? If you think about it, it's the same thing that determines whether nonprofit results are great. It's about comparison.

The Power of Comparison

Comparison is something universal, even central, to human behavior. The social psychologist Leon Festinger is probably best known as the father of cognitive dissonance, the practice of holding two conflicting beliefs at the same time. But Festinger's early work in the 1950s introduced what he called social comparison theory: the insight that as social beings our self-assessments are heavily influenced by others.

In the decades since, researchers have validated the core of Festinger's theory. In 2014, for example, academics across three different studies found that the influence of social comparison is so powerful that even when people set out to evaluate themselves using mastery-based goals, ultimately they are still more influenced by comparison-based information.

Here's a familiar example. Imagine yourself getting a 75 percent grade on your first physics quiz in college, a disappointing C minus. How would you feel? If you're interested in mastery, you would probably feel deflated and unsatisfied with your performance. But then imagine you come to class and find out your grade was the highest in a class of 40 students. Now, how do you feel? Elated? Proud? What changed? What changed is the overpowering effect of social comparison information (or TOESCI, as some researchers call it).

Social comparison explains other surprising results, too. For example, it explains why in experimental settings some people tend to prefer less money if it means their income exceeds that of their peers. That is, they would give up greater wealth for the sole purpose of avoiding *relative* income inferiority.

This should make us rethink the supposed supremacy of the profit motive, per se, in driving success. Of course, wealth and profit represent one of the most useful measures for comparing ourselves to others, but when it comes to the motivation money can inspire, it serves more as a means rather than an end.

This is all good news for nonprofit leaders because it means the marginal difference between one firm's returns and another's is analogous to the marginal difference between two nonprofit leaders' achievements. The trick is to set aside the nonprofit conundrum of trying to quantify that difference and instead look at how we might increase the volume, relevance, and impact of social comparison information among our sector.

The Role of Social Comparison in Nonprofit Success

It's clear that in order for comparison to occur, nonprofit leaders need peers. Less well known is what social psychology can teach us about the type of peers we should seek and the type of environments most conducive to increasing the quality of social comparison-based information. For the ambitious nonprofit leader, learning and applying those insights can mean the difference between maintaining modest success and carving out new standards of excellence.

Richard Durana is the head of a nonprofit think tank in Slovakia. After spending four intensive days at Atlas Network's Europe Liberty Forum in Copenhagen, he told me, "I call these events *mindquakes*. Meeting the brightest minds in the movement always pumps new inspiration and energy into my veins."

Richard's inventive word, "mindquakes," captures perfectly what can happen when you get the right mix of people together. But it's not all serendipity. Researchers from the University of Michigan and University of Notre Dame explain there are three dimensions that have been shown to affect the level of competitive juices among peers: relevance, similarity, and closeness. How relevant are the peers' points of comparison to their success? How similar are they to each other? How personally close are they in their relationship? In my observation, many think tank leaders intuitively emphasize those dimensions when they reflect on their experience at Atlas Network events.

Joe Lehman is president of a think tank in Michigan. He and his organization are widely admired as successful examples of the kind of work they do. If you ask Joe, though, part of the secret to that success is his practice of seeking out the kind of peers who represent relevant dimensions of comparison. Specifically, he explains, "The most effective way for me to improve is to surround myself with people who are better than I am, at something. That routinely happens in CEO exchanges."

Foundation for Government Accountability's founder and CEO Tarren Bragdon reinforced the benefits of similarity when he wrote me to say, "Atlas Network's CEO Summit is a must attend event for me. I learn, get inspired, and get challenged by my peers *who understand my world like no one else* [emphasis mine]." Another think tank leader, London-based Mark Littlewood, is general director of the Institute of Economic Affairs. He underscored the importance of creating *closeness* via networking when he assessed his time at an Atlas Network event saying, "I have never come across any event on the planet at which I have made so many vital personal and professional friendships amongst my peers."

Choosing Your Peers

These three dimensions—relevance, similarity, and closeness—represent an opportunity for nonprofit leaders to assess how motivating their peer group is in driving their own success. Luckily, unsatisfactory assessments need not be fatal.

In his book, *Choosing the Right Pond: Human Behavior and the Quest for Status*, economist Robert Frank observes that because we can largely choose to whom we compare ourselves, we have the power to influence whether or not our chosen "pond" dulls our drive to succeed or inspires us to achieve even more. We've all heard the expression "big fish, little pond" to describe the relative standing of someone who, if compared to a wider pool of peers in a much bigger pond, might not rank as highly as they do at home.

Ultimately, no one wants to be a victim of "big fish, little pond" syndrome, believing you are already the best you can be simply because you avoid comparing yourself to fish in bigger ponds.

Using the three dimensions to avoid that mistake, nonprofit leaders can ask themselves:

- If I am determined to achieve even more than I am now, what peers can I choose that are most relevant for a motivating comparison—and from whom can I learn the most?
- Are those peers similar enough to me that my comparisons will truly inspire in me a desire to try to outperform them?
- What am I doing to develop meaningful, personal relationships with those peers, and am I willing to invest the necessary time to get closer to them?

Atlas Network's Coach, Compete, Celebrate! Model

Through the lens of social comparison, the global network of think tanks represents an incredible resource for ambitious nonprofit leaders to engage. At the same time, those individual dimensions are not the only levers available for increasing comparison and competitiveness. Organizations like Atlas Network are also in the position to foster those productive behaviors through what researchers call "situational" factors such as: *incentive structures* like zero-sum games; *proximity to a standard* dynamics, whereby a fine point is put on differences in performance through ranking; *enhanced competition*, a phenomenon that occurs as narrower bands of peers are formed to try to outperform each other; and *social category fault lines*, where forms of self-identity become rallying cries for competitiveness (e.g., Americans versus Europeans).

Atlas Network developed its *Coach, Compete, Celebrate!* model based largely on those factors in combination with other insights from our research on networks and innovation diffusion. In the absence of a profit margin, we think those insights taken together represent the most effective strategy for fueling the powerful effects you can expect from social comparison.

Specifically, we convene peer groups for training, networking, competitions, and awards. Each year, we host regional Liberty Forums in Africa, Asia, Europe, and Latin America as well as our global Liberty Forum & Freedom Dinner, each with all the key insights of social comparison and innovation diffusion integrated into our strategy.

What's more, award-winning projects become the basis for case studies used to continually update the curriculum of our training programs so peers are engaging the latest success stories to inspire and motivate new ambitions. We also bring cross-sections of CEOs to new regions to generate new peer groups across diverse organizations and to establish new personal friendships around the world.

One of the ways we validate our model is to compare the year-over-year increase in the quality of the six finalist projects for the annual Templeton Freedom Award. Each year, the caliber of applicants and finalists leaps forward as the network-wide definition of what it means to be "good" at this kind of work is continually raised to new standards of excellence. We can hardly contain our enthusiasm each year as we carefully review, and become inspired by, the incredible achievements of our partners that consistently outpace the high watermarks of the past.

Just the Beginning

Our experience makes clear that nonprofit leaders are just as capable of being innovative and results-oriented as for-profit leaders. The key is for our network of partners and philanthropists to embrace together the power of social comparison as our industry's most important and most powerful strategic alternative to profit-based measurements of success. This strategy is working. It's incredible to see how quickly we are making progress—and, as I would say to that younger version of myself admiring that first set of waterfalls, just wait till you see what's coming next.

SECTION III
Case Studies on Property Rights

Without secure property rights, those in poverty are not only severely limited in what they can achieve economically, but they are also vulnerable to violation of all other rights—political, human, and civil. Take, for example, the 2010 case of Mohamed Bouazizi, the humble Tunisian vegetable seller who, after years of being harassed by local government officials seeking bribes, set himself on fire in public protest. His last words were, "How do you expect me to make a living?"

Like Mohamed, many people earning low incomes suffer from insecure property rights. They may lack formal title to their homes or land, or their wares and money are too easily subject to government seizure without cause. This can be a problem in countries both rich and poor. Only where property ownership is secure and government is restrained to follow the rule of law will we see more people free to achieve economic success.

Versions of the case studies in this section are available at AtlasNetwork.org.

Fighting Government Abuses of Power

Institute for Justice, United States

Introduction

The Institute for Justice (IJ) is a nonprofit public-interest law firm located in Arlington, Virginia, in the United States. It describes itself on its website as "the national law firm for liberty litigating to limit the size and scope of government power and to ensure that all Americans have the right to control their own destinies as free and responsible members of society."

The organization was founded by William H. "Chip" Mellor and Clint Bolick in 1991 and has grown to a staff size of more than 100 employees. IJ operates from its headquarters near Washington, D.C., and also maintains offices in six other locations throughout the country. Today, the firm is led by Scott Bullock, who joined IJ at its founding, with Mellor serving as chairman of the board of directors. Bullock has a law degree from the University of Pittsburgh and a bachelor's degree in economics from Grove City College.

IJ categorizes its work around four "pillars of freedom": economic liberty, school choice, free speech, and property rights. It boasts a 70-percent success rate in winning cases,[1] typically representing individuals such as small-business owners, parents of school-aged children, and property owners.

Beginning in 2006, IJ formed what it calls the Strategic Research Program, a department designed to provide original and rigorous social science research to support IJ's litigation efforts.

Dick Carpenter and Lisa Knepper, directors of strategic research, lead the Strategic Research Program. Carpenter has a background in social science research and education (including higher education and K–12), having earned his doctorate from the University of

Colorado. Before joining the Strategic Research Program, Knepper was director of communications for IJ. She is a graduate of the Ohio State University, where she majored in economics and political science. Also on the Strategic Research Program team are a senior research analyst, two research analysts, and a research editor, for a total of six in the program, five of whom work at IJ's headquarters.

Project Narrative

In the 1990s, IJ started litigating cases related to eminent domain, which is the governmental power to take private land or other property for public use. IJ represented property owners whose land was being taken by the government for private use under the justification that the takings had a public purpose (e.g., redevelopment, attracting jobs to the area, increasing the tax base, etc.). The media attention received by those cases triggered a steady stream of phone calls to IJ from property owners around the country who claimed they were also victims of eminent domain abuse.

Public opinion is an important part of IJ's strategy, in part because it maintains that judges, like most people, are aware of issues in the public eye. A critical piece of IJ's public-interest mission involves shifting public opinion in favor of more freedom-friendly policies. To do that, IJ knows that it's important to tell the stories of the specific individuals who are affected by the destructive policies it fights in each of its cases. Audiences are more likely to become passionate about an issue and engage with[1] it when it has a human face, and IJ's clients provide natural subjects.

In the case of eminent domain, though, the IJ team knew that individual stories alone would not earn them the level of coverage they needed. "We knew that to raise the profile of this issue, we needed to demonstrate this was a national problem," explained Knepper. "It wasn't enough, though, to say we were getting a lot of phone calls; we needed to put a number to it."

Mellor turned to Dana Berliner, then a senior attorney for the firm. Today, Berliner is senior vice president and litigation director.

Berliner and a small team spent more than a year searching for any instances of eminent domain use for private development, sourcing news accounts and court records around the country. The result was a landmark publication, *Public Power, Private Gain*, released in April 2003. It documented more than 10,000 cases of properties threatened by eminent domain abuse in a five-year period.

This shocking number led to a major story on the CBS News program *60 Minutes*, a level of exposure that Knepper believes increased the likelihood that one of IJ's now-famous cases, *Kelo v. City of New London*, would reach the U.S. Supreme Court. The court ruled against IJ's clients, including Susette Kelo, in 2005, but Justice O'Connor cited *Public Power, Private Gain* in her dissenting opinion, pointing to specific cases that IJ had documented to show how no property is safe under the court's rationale.

The case had two silver linings. First, it triggered a national outcry that raised awareness about the issue of eminent domain to an unprecedented level. Second, the court suggested in its majority opinion that individual state governments could tighten the laws governing the use of eminent domain in their states. IJ immediately began to lead a major coalition effort to reform state laws around the country, with much success.

By pairing individual, emotionally engaging stories with robust, nationwide data, IJ brought the issue of eminent domain to popular attention. The isolated stories could no longer be dismissed as anomalies, and the numbers were humanized with the faces of real clients affected, so IJ's target audiences paid attention and became engaged.

Mellor realized this was a winning combination and sought to institutionalize it within IJ. He created the Strategic Research Program in 2006 and, knowing that communications would be central to the development of all research products, he asked Lisa Knepper to transition from her role as director of communications to be part of the Strategic Research Program's leadership team. IJ then hired Dick Carpenter to work alongside Knepper.

The research team's first project focused on economic liberty. Shortly after that, they turned their attention toward a property

rights issue that was then largely unknown outside of the law enforcement and legal communities—civil asset forfeiture. IJ describes
civil asset forfeiture as:

> *A mechanism by which law enforcement agencies can seize and
> keep property on the mere suspicion that it is connected to a crime.
> In contrast to criminal forfeiture, where property is taken only
> after a criminal conviction, civil forfeiture allows law enforcement
> to take property from innocent people who have never been formal-
> ly accused of a crime, let alone convicted of one.*

At the time, IJ had just begun to address the issue of civil asset
forfeiture, filing an amicus brief in one case and litigating another.
Bullock had lost a case in New Jersey representing a former sheriff
whose car was taken, but he had also raised the profile of the case
by telling the story of Carol Thomas of Millville, New Jersey, whose
teenaged son had been arrested on a drug charge while driving
her car without permission. Bullock managed to get her car back,
but the systemic practice of forfeiture was upheld. The experience
helped to crystallize the key problems with most forfeiture laws: the
financial incentive for police to abuse their power and the reverse
burden of proof property owners must meet to get their assets back.

Essentially, property owners are denied basic due process rights
and are deemed guilty until they prove their innocence. IJ knew
its goal was to see civil asset forfeiture eliminated, and for revenue
from criminal asset forfeiture to be rerouted to a neutral fund that
would eliminate the strong incentive for policing agencies to abuse
their power.

In 2007, Carpenter and Knepper met with Bullock, then a senior
attorney, to address this question: What could IJ do to lay a foundation for future forfeiture efforts, illustrate the extent of the problem,
and shine a light on civil asset forfeiture? The team could point to
examples of news stories covering individual cases of civil asset forfeiture, but without comprehensive data, it was hard to argue there
was a systemic problem.

After conducting a literature review, the team set out to test
whether variations in state laws correlated with the use and abuse

of civil asset forfeiture. It soon became clear, though, that obtaining the data would be difficult and, in many states, impossible because of poor record keeping. Even in states where reporting was required, it was sometimes simply ignored.

Here the team turned to three external researchers that they discovered during the literature review process: Marian Williams, Jefferson Holcomb, and Tomislav Kovandzic. Each had a doctorate and had all published on the topic. They suggested that the team also look into the issue of equitable sharing, a practice whereby states can turn to the federal government to adopt a forfeiture case or work jointly to seize assets. Police departments in states that have stronger protections for property owners can use this loophole to keep up to 80 percent of the revenue from the forfeiture.

Not only did this revelation improve upon the initial research question that IJ had planned to pursue, but it also solved the data problem: all equitable-sharing activity by the states is recorded in a central database at the Department of Justice.

For the next three years, the Strategic Research Program team, including the external researchers they hired, collected all the data available from states and the Department of Justice, using Freedom of Information requests when necessary. This effort yielded tens of thousands of documents, all of which needed to be coded and organized in spreadsheets by IJ's team.

In March 2010, the team published *Policing for Profit*, the first national report with comprehensive data on just how common and lucrative civil asset forfeiture can be for government agencies. For example, the report revealed that in 2008, for the first time, the Department of Justice held more than $1 billion from civil asset forfeiture. It also confirmed that equitable sharing incentivized agencies in states with stricter laws to turn to the federal government more frequently.

The report itself did not immediately attract a lot of attention, in part because the issue was so little known. Moreover, "The national report can't do it all," Carpenter explained. "Judges and reporters want to contextualize the problem in their state." So, while IJ's litigation teams found new clients and began filing suits, the Strategic Research Program team got busy creating specific state reports to supplement the national study.

"But the national [report] was so important; no one had taken the time to describe the problem, and so [the national report] made clear there was a serious problem," Carpenter continued. "And then the state reports confirmed that, in places where our litigation was happening, it was also a problem there. The judge couldn't say, 'well, that may be an issue at the national level, but here in our state things are different.'"

Here is where persistence pays off, Knepper points out. The media began to take notice. "Because we had legal information on every state, and we had the federal data, it gave every state a news hook," she said. It also gave national journalists a complete story to dig into.

In August 2013, the *New Yorker* magazine published a compelling, long-form article about civil forfeiture by staff writer Sarah Stillman, quoting IJ's legislative counsel Lee McGrath. Michael Sallah, then of the *Washington Post*, had covered specific cases of forfeiture when he worked for the *Miami Herald* (to which he has since returned), so he was familiar with the issue. After reading *Policing for Profit*, he reached out to the IJ team to learn more. He subsequently published, with co-writers, a widely read six-part series on asset forfeiture in the *Post* beginning in September 2014. The *Post*'s series summary uses this description:

> *In recent years, thousands of people have had cash confiscated by police without being charged with crimes. The Post looks at the police culture behind the seizures and the people who were forced to fight the government to get their money back.*

IJ was cited as a key source. In May 2015, journalist Conor Friedersdorf wrote a piece for *The Atlantic* titled "The Injustice of Civil Asset Forfeiture," which linked directly to *Policing for Profit*.

This blitz of media coverage was the tipping point in elevating the topic across the country. "We weren't just spending 10 minutes on the phone with reporters here and there," Carpenter said. "We were spending hours and hours meeting with reporters, walking them through the data and helping them understand the extent of this problem."

By elevating the issue and providing attorneys with intellectual ammunition, the Strategic Research Program team had made litigation a more effective tool for achieving justice and reform. For example, IJ won a judgment in Georgia that required state agencies to comply with reporting laws.

The team also helped to trigger reform efforts at all levels of government. In January 2015, U.S. Attorney General Eric Holder announced that the Department of Justice (DOJ) would curb some of its civil asset forfeiture practices, particularly one type of equitable sharing. IJ accessed the DOJ database to assess the implications of this policy change, and discovered most current seizures would be unaffected. In response to this type of criticism, the DOJ issued additional guidelines to provide stricter definitions for eligibility, but IJ remains vigilant in its efforts to further limit government abuse.

In November 2015, IJ released the second edition of *Policing for Profit,* and it continues to take on new cases and new research angles. For example, one of its clients in Michigan saw all his business capital seized from his bank because the deposit amounts consistently fell below a threshold that would require federal reporting. When done intentionally to avoid reporting, this practice is called "structuring" and can make federal agents suspicious of your activities. IJ's client, however, was not intentionally structuring, which government officials could have discerned if they had engaged in a simple investigation. In response, IJ has issued a new report, *Seize First, Ask Questions Later,* demonstrating an ongoing commitment to respond in a timely manner to new developments.

Key Insights

The model of the Strategic Research Program team has proven effective at elevating issues and illustrating key concepts that are relevant to IJ's litigation efforts. By designing research to meet specific communications and litigation goals, without sacrificing quality (research projects are often painstaking and time consuming), the Strategic Research Program team is able to define its framework for making decisions.

On Collaboration

Carpenter describes the research development process as collaborative. Within the Strategic Research Program team, Knepper provides early editing and production leadership. Beyond the Strategic Research Program team, Carpenter estimates that, on average, draft research is shared with IJ's communications team at least six weeks before publication. The integrity of the research methodology is never on the table, but the communications team does provide additional ideas for how best to explain the findings, which stories best illustrate the issue, and which language will be both accurate but also clear and accessible to IJ's audience. This feedback influences the final text.

Most research is related to litigation, so the Strategic Research Program team works with IJ's attorneys early in the process to brainstorm critical arguments, anticipate counterarguments, and identify potential gaps in knowledge about an issue among judges, reporters, and the public.

IJ's teams work within what they call business units. Those include strategic research, litigation, legislation, communications, and activism. Knepper described a fluid and collaborative process across business units to advance specific issues or projects. Input and coordination is critical, and although IJ relies to some degree on managerial oversight, it more predominately cultivates a good-faith effort that is usually cited as a credit to the organization's culture. "Not only is everyone expected to pitch in and help out, but people really want to," Knepper said. "I think they've seen it work and they know that we are most effective when we are working together." She added that although IJ does not operate in an overly hierarchical way, the example has to start from the top, and the quality of the culture has to be carefully maintained through the hiring process.

On Identifying Your Audience

Knepper defines the IJ audience broadly as any reasonably informed, average American. IJ also operates an activism arm, and the Strategic Research Program team wants all active citizens to engage the research with ease. Internally, Carpenter said, they call it the "Mom Test." If your explanation of the problem and the solution won't make sense to your mom, keep working on it. Jargon or overly academic writing should be reserved for journals, not popular or even professional audiences.

On Obtaining Government Data

Carpenter recommends that someone on every public policy organization's team become an expert in Freedom of Information Act laws, or the equivalent in other countries where such laws exist. He said that this not only optimizes efforts to obtain government information but also confers credibility with judges and other government agencies, particularly in the face of lackluster cooperation or hostility.

On Messaging

Carpenter said it can be counterproductive to focus on vilifying individuals in the government. This may lead to the erroneous conclusion that simply replacing the people in charge will solve the problem. Instead, he said that IJ's message focuses on changing the rules—change incentives, change behavior.

Knepper emphasized the importance of including the stories of real people in messaging. Most audiences are more likely to engage if they can identify a specific victim, which triggers a stronger emotional response than statistics alone. Those stories are included, with imagery, in research reports and paired with data showing that the story is not an isolated incident. That is a powerful combination. Both are critical to success; one enhances the other.

On Measurement

IJ as an organization focuses on winning lawsuits, but it also seeks favorable settlements and desirable legislative reform. The communications department carefully monitors media coverage, and the Strategic Research Program team has begun to look specifically at media coverage that references or relies on their research. They also monitor whether their research played a meaningful role in a judge's decision. The Strategic Research Program team has a secondary goal of inspiring more research in their chosen focus areas, and part of their strategy to achieve this is to publish academic versions of their research in journals.

Discussion Questions

- Is the IJ relationship between research and communications optimal? What advantages or disadvantages can you see?
- Sometimes, IJ spends years on research projects. It also persists over lengthy time horizons to promote research in the media. How does your organization make decisions about allocating resources in this way? What are the tradeoffs? Do those tradeoffs change depending on staff size and budget?
- IJ conducts litigation and then develops research topics that strategically advance those litigation efforts. How do you select topics for research? Even if your organization does not initiate litigation, how do you identify desirable outcomes to help frame your decision-making?
- How do you balance hierarchy with collaboration in your office in order to optimize outcomes? Do you think about your organizational culture when you make a new hire?
- What are the individual stories you can tell about the people affected by the issues that your organization tackles? Is this part of your organization's model for research and communications?

Restoring Title for Victims of Apartheid

Free Market Foundation, South Africa

Introduction

The Free Market Foundation (FMF) is a South African think tank founded in 1975 to promote and foster the classical liberal principles of an open society, the rule of law, personal liberty, and economic freedom as fundamental components of its advocacy of human rights and democracy. One of the founders, Leon Louw, is a South African intellectual entrepreneur and life-long property rights activist. His interest in property rights came from an early personal experience while working at a law firm in Johannesburg. According to Louw, "Every day I saw and occasionally bought food from an elderly black woman who sold fruit on the sidewalk outside our law offices. One day I saw the police kick her basket of fruit into the street and chase her down around the corner where they caught and arrested her; they threw her violently into their police van, and drove off. I dropped what I was doing and followed. They took her to [a] central Johannesburg police station where I spent the rest of the day trying to get her released."

This anecdote describes the spirit and motivation behind both FMF and its Khaya Lam (My House) Land Reform project, an initiative to return freehold land titles to survivors of South Africa's Apartheid. As Temba Nolutshungu, co-director of FMF, explains, "I still remember a time when black South Africans could not even conceive of owning land."

Enacted in 1913, the Natives Land Act prohibited black people from buying or owning land and also forbade them from being tenant farmers on land owned by white people. Post-Apartheid reforms in the 1990s sought to reverse this oppressive legacy by ending the prohibition and making it possible for tenants of government property to obtain freehold title to their homes.

The new law, however, has not been sufficient to trigger the change that Nolutshungu describes. The vast majority of title conversion candidates today remain either unaware or distrustful of the opportunity. FMF started the Khaya Lam project to bridge this divide and to secure titles for as many conversion candidates as possible.

Today, FMF is led by executive director Louw and co-directors Eustace Davie, Temba Nolutshungu, and Jasson Urbach and employs 10 full-time and three part-time employees with an annual operating budget of roughly US$650,000. Its board of advisors includes the highly regarded economists Deepak Lal and Israel Kirzner.

Project Narrative

The goal of the Khaya Lam Land Reform project is to secure title for previously disenfranchised South Africans. FMF estimates there are as many as 7 million such candidates, an immense figure. To turn legal rights into reality, the FMF team knew they needed to test a new model for facilitating land title conversion on a smaller scale, using the results to inspire further cooperation and replication throughout the country.

The team developed the initial goal of converting 3,000 municipally owned rental houses into freehold titles through a pilot project. They believe this will not only encourage economic growth in the communities affected but also convince government leaders to extend the title conversion policy to all 7 million of South Africa's government-owned rental houses.

The team identified the Ngwathe municipal area of the Free State province for the pilot project. Ngwathe includes approximately 17,000 candidate properties and has a municipal council led by a majority party that largely supported land titling at its founding.

The FMF team had gotten to know a retired farmer in Ngwathe named Perry Feldman, who later became a project manager for Khaya Lam. Feldman made introductions to local officials, and

Louw made a request for a meeting with the municipal council in order to present the FMF plan, explaining the anticipated economic benefits for the community. The council voted and approved the plan, including a provision that the council would not "impose pre-emptive conditions that restrict the rights of what black residents may do with their land."

According to Nolutshungu, this provision was important because, "In a free market, there has to be voluntary exchange, personal choice and private property. Only when government accepts these principles as sacrosanct can South Africa realize a peaceful, socio-economic revolution that will result in the economic uplifting of the greatest number of people."

The council was not only supportive, but, according to FMF project coordinator Gail Day, it promised to provide "a one-stop-shop to deal with and minimize formalities and red tape." Because of this reduced administrative burden, and because FMF had negotiated a bulk rate with attorneys, the project was able to reduce the average cost per title at the time from US$348, a formidable sum for local residents, to about US$122. With an average property value for candidate homes in Ngwathe of US$8,000, this represented a compelling value proposition.

Another FMF representative, Jeanette Mpondo, then set up an office in Ngwathe in cooperation with the council and served as a land reform liaison officer to work directly with potential beneficiaries as she helped them prepare documentation for their title applications.

Setting up the office in Ngwathe was a critical step. The FMF team quickly learned the importance of local relationships and building trust. Mpondo maintained office hours, but spent much of her time working in the community to better understand residents' views. This helped FMF get up to speed quickly on local concerns and adjust accordingly.

For example, local residents did not trust the attorneys that FMF had initially hired to serve them. Because they were from out of town, they were seen as foreigners and not committed to local residents' best interests. In their place, FMF hired local attorneys

65

who understood local attitudes and who had existing relationships with residents.

The team also gained a deeper appreciation for the role of marketing and outreach, particularly the need to explain the benefits of titling. For some, the opportunity to own property is innately attractive. For others, the benefits are less obvious and the administrative hurdles and accompanying costs arouse suspicion.

To combat this, the FMF team developed a multipronged marketing strategy. First, they went door-to-door, introducing themselves to candidate residents and explaining the economic benefits of ownership. Mpondo was also given a weekly slot on the local radio station to speak to residents about the benefits of titling and to invite applications when new donor funds became available for titling.

Second, they held informational events to explain the application process and to provide an overview of ownership benefits (opportunity to sell, incentive to improve, and ability to access credit markets). Those events also provided residents the chance to ask questions such as, "Will my children really be able to inherit my property?"

Third, they organized functions at which larger donors could personally present the title deeds to the new homeowners they sponsored. For instance, representatives of the First National Bank presented title deeds to 200 successful applicants in the school hall in Tumahole township. FMF also invited project donors to witness the transfer of title and to get to know the people their funds had benefited. For example, FMF held a titling ceremony for Maria Mothupi, who was 99 years old at the time. For Mothupi, the benefits of her new title were clear: She would now have something to leave her grandchildren. She also said she would invest in a few improvements on the property. As Nolutshungu notes, "for many black South Africans [land titling] is a healing process."

Donor Tersia Cook joined the ceremony and celebrated with Mothupi. Cook said she made the donation in lieu of a birthday present to her brother and was so glad she did so. She later threw a 100th birthday party for Mothupi in January 2016, with FMF in attendance.

The FMF team shared Mothupi's story in marketing materials and generated some media attention. By using the title transfer ceremony as an opportunity to both galvanize donors and expose neighbors and friends to the opportunity, FMF was able to accelerate its rate of applicants and expand its funding.

Fourth, the team also secured the vocal support of popular government leaders such as Free State Premier Ace Magashule and Ngwathe Executive Mayor Joey Mochela. Those leaders helped to draw media to titling ceremonies, where reporters could meet the individuals and families benefiting from the project. Those stories helped to engage key audiences and energize them for this cause.

Fifth, FMF reached out to local businesses, including banks and farms, explaining the significance of the work they were doing. Some farms began sponsoring their workers' titles. Through word of mouth and media attention, other businesses began calling FMF to ask how they could get involved.

For example, a nationwide hardware company has sponsored 54 title transfers in Ngwathe and promised to carry out titling in every area where it operates stores. A fruit exporter promised to assist all its 100 or so workers to obtain title to their homes. A large steel manufacturer in the Johannesburg metropolitan area is exploring the feasibility of helping 5,000 of its workers obtain title to their homes. Those opportunities are helping to pave the way for expansion beyond the pilot project and into other municipalities.

By early 2016, the pilot project had secured 870 land titles in Ngwathe, with another 300 in the pipeline. There has been an increase in donor interest in titling in other areas, too, with contributions and pledges received for 1,700 title transfers, mainly in the Cape Town area.

FMF has demonstrated that for every US$100,000 in funding it secures for direct project expenses, it is able to generate approximately US$6.7 million in capital for low-income South Africans. This translates into potential for loans for education expenses, new businesses, and property improvements, as well as opportunities for inheritance and relocation.

Key Insights

On Participation

FMF developed a deeper appreciation through this project for the importance of knowing its audience. The local residents of Ngwathe did not immediately jump at the chance to obtain title through FMF's project. In fact, earning the trust and enthusiasm of eligible residents continues to require effort. Some do not believe such an opportunity could be real. Others do not see the benefit, or think it is not worth the effort to apply. This illuminates a broader insight about helping others: It is crucial to understand the perspective, desires, and tradeoffs of those you desire to help. Their knowledge is the most relevant for the decisions they must make. Those decisions must be made voluntarily. FMF was able to adjust its efforts to better account for local needs. By using local attorneys, relocating key staff to work daily among the eligible residents, and working through local bodies, FMF was better able to discover a productive model for success.

On Getting Started

There are an estimated 7 million candidates for FMF's project. That is a daunting number. By developing a manageable pilot project, FMF was able to demonstrate viability while building its model with flexibility. Starting a project on a large scale can be risky, particularly if the experience of executing the project informs significant changes in program design. For more on this, read Eric Ries's book *The Lean Startup*.

On Funding

FMF wants to see all candidates given the opportunity to learn about and consider converting to land titles, but it knows that the current funding model will not be able to meet the full scale of what is possible. For this reason, it is important that FMF continue to track and demonstrate the benefits of titling, particularly among those who have benefited from Khaya Lam. Even US$122 can be a large sum for many in South Africa, so FMF hopes to see enough appreciation for the upside of titling that candidates will begin finding their own ways to raise the funds for their title conversions, either through savings or borrowing. In addition, the employer model, whereby companies sponsor their workers' land titles, has considerable promise. Planning ahead for subsequent project phases can help ease transitions to shifts in the funding model.

On Messaging

Understanding your audience is key. In South Africa, some economic terms are heavily politicized and loaded with contentious meanings. "We did not once talk about capitalism; we went in and talked about titles and property," Davie noted. "That's it." By focusing on its audience and not its own interests, FMF was better able to articulate the benefits of the project in ways that resonated and produced results. FMF also consistently presents itself as a nonpartisan organization that is sincerely committed to achieving justice for those harmed by the Apartheid era. As a result, they have been able to bridge partisan divides and work with a diversity of allies.

Discussion Questions

- List the audiences that one of your programs is intended to serve. What are the benefits they will realize if you are successful? How can you communicate those benefits effectively to those audiences in a way that will resonate and engage them in your cause? Will jargon that is associated with the ideas of liberty enhance or confuse your message?
- Identify a new or upcoming project in your organization. How can you test your model without overinvesting in features that may not be successful?
- Are there opportunities to bring your donors and the beneficiaries of your work together to meet and learn from each other? Draft a plan for such an occasion and brainstorm ways to ensure a memorable experience. Could this also serve as a media opportunity?
- Are there any opportunities to help accelerate the benefits of existing public policy in your area?

Restoring Land Rights for Small Farmers

EasyBusiness, Ukraine

Introduction

Founded in 2014, the mission of EasyBusiness is to improve Ukraine's business climate by providing economic research and independent policy recommendations based on the principles of free markets and competition. EasyBusiness' policy focus includes land market reform, investment and business climate improvement, and facilitating innovation among Ukrainian startups.

When the Ukrainian government decided to ignore calls for property reform, innovative leaders formed EasyBusiness to create a vehicle for researchers, litigators, and everyday citizens to open up the market for property owners to be able to freely buy and sell farmland that had been restricted previously.

The group's founders were originally on a team of government deregulators where they urged the government to prioritize the property rights reform, particularly to end the moratorium on agricultural land sales. Their recommendations were ignored, so they eventually formed EasyBusiness, first on a volunteer basis, and took their fight to the courts.

At the same time, they also launched a user-friendly online platform to give Ukrainian landowners the tools they needed to wage their own campaigns with their local officials and also with the European Court of Human Rights, or ECHR, to create widespread, bottom-up pressure for reform.

"Courts can become very helpful partners in supporting important reforms," said Andrew Shpakov, CEO of EasyBusiness. "They are usually seen as independent, and external parties that are capable of presenting an unbiased view of the problem in question.

In our case, it worked out perfectly. Both the public and politicians saw that the necessity of the free farmland market is not a factional demand but a direct requirement of the recognized international body that protects property rights. This decision made it easier to advocate for the implementation of the land reform."

Here's how EasyBusiness' work opened up land markets in Ukraine:

- **A new precedent.** EasyBusiness' efforts led to a favorable ruling from the ECHR, providing a credible precedent for the 7 million affected landowners to assert their rights. The think tank estimates the liberalization of this market may bring as much as US$100 billion to the economy in the long term. It also estimates the moratorium prevents anywhere from US$500 million to $600 million of foreign direct investment and roughly US$10 billion of potential GDP growth per year.
- **Change from within.** Shortly following the court's decision, 69 members of the Ukrainian Parliament submitted a case to the Constitutional Court of Ukraine to admit that the moratorium violates the Ukrainian Constitution. The Ministry of Justice in Ukraine also convened a working group—that included EasyBusiness—and charged the group with developing an effective mechanism for launching a formal farmland market in Ukraine.
- **The full force of a reform movement.** EasyBusiness performed comprehensive policy research, built a coalition of experts from the ground up, and has already aided more than 500 Ukrainian landowners through their online platform, mobilizing a powerful brain trust and grassroots movement.

Project Narrative

Ukraine ranks last in economic freedom among the 44 European countries, according to the Heritage Foundation's 2019 Index of Economic Freedom. One of the freedoms most infringed upon is property rights. About 7 million landowners in Ukraine are legally prohibited from selling their land, making Ukraine the only democratic state where people are barred from freely disposing of their property.

This 15 percent of the population owns 70 percent of the land, much of which is underutilized. The moratorium on the sale of agricultural land in the country has been a hot-button issue for many years until very recently, when Kyiv-based EasyBusiness backed a successful lawsuit in the ECHR.

Like many policies that ultimately cause harm, restrictions on Ukraine's farmland market was born of good intentions. Land was given out as reparations for suffering under the former Soviet communist regime, and the new government created laws that prohibited that land from being sold as a way to protect the new land owners from pressure to sell. But years later, one of the byproducts is that many landowners own parcels of land they can't afford to maintain—but which they also can't do anything else with. They can't sell, and they can't use their property as collateral in commercial ventures. They've become "land poor."

Several Atlas Network partners have engaged in this issue in Ukraine, and EasyBusiness has been a leading voice in providing credible paths toward land reform and in popularizing the idea of a free market for farmland. Over four years, the group developed a comprehensive policy research program, a roadmap for land market reform, and facilitated a broad communications strategy to reach both experts and everyday Ukrainians who were not familiar with the issue.

The group also launched www.farmland.in.ua/, a website to help landowners file applications to the ECHR challenging the constitutionality of Ukraine's land sales ban. Over 500 applications were submitted through the platform, two of which were actually considered by the ECHR, where EasyBusiness then became a third party to provide expert economic and legislative background as an independent think tank.

In May 2018, the two Ukrainian landowners won their case at the ECHR against the Ukrainian government. Soon after ECHR's ruling, 69 Members of the Ukrainian Parliament submitted a case to the Constitutional Court of Ukraine, conceding that the country's so-called moratorium on farmland sales violates the Ukrainian Constitution.

EasyBusiness estimates that reforming Ukraine's ban on land sales may bring as much as US$100 billion to the economy in the long term. It also estimates the moratorium prevents anywhere from US$500 million to $600 million of foreign direct investment and roughly US$10 billion of potential GDP growth per year.

Due to the moratorium on free farmland sales in Ukraine, 7 million farmland owners (comprising 15 percent of Ukraine's total population) who own 28 million hectares of farmland plots (70 percent of Ukraine's total farmland) cannot freely dispose of their farmland plots. This human rights violation means Ukraine is the only democratic state worldwide (along with Venezuela, Cuba, Tajikistan, and North Korea) where the moratorium on farmland sales still exists.

To change this, EasyBusiness faced a steep uphill battle with many challenges:

- A lack of awareness among local authorities and landowners regarding the benefits of a free farmland market for the economy and landowners themselves (only 18.8 percent of Ukrainians are well informed regarding the reform specifics)
- Biased public perception of the reform, caused by aggressive media campaigns from populist political parties (only 32.4 percent of Ukrainians supported the land reform at the outset of the EasyBusiness campaign)
- Lack of political support for land reform overall and abolishment of a moratorium on free farmland sales, in particular, that is correlated with an influx of populism in Ukraine.

Despite these challenges, EasyBusiness found innovative ways to turn the tide in favor of reform and freedom.

Key Insights

On shaping public opinion

"Generally speaking, the land reform campaign was a special case that combined low public support for a free market and reluctance from politicians to take any active measures," said Andrew Shpakov, CEO of EasyBusiness. "The public did not understand the tangible benefits of the reform and were scared that 'foreign interests will buy out all Ukrainian farmland.' Meanwhile, the politicians mostly abstained from the land matters as it was politically toxic and could harm their political image."

What to do when you're working against a well-established—but incorrect—narrative? EasyBusiness started by establishing a new baseline, armed with facts and data.

Their research started with an analysis of 60 countries to explain the benefits of land reform systems. EasyBusiness' team became the "myth busters" who were uncovering the truth about free markets. They showed how everyday Ukrainians are harmed by the ban and how a free market would create massive economic benefits for Ukraine and its people.

This new research garnered a lot of media attention and moved government influencers, but EasyBusiness still had a long way to go convincing the general public, specifically the landowners who would benefit most from reform. So the group launched a new initiative to mobilize open-minded landowners to appeal to the ECHR.

A new website, farmland.in.ua, allowed landowners to file applications to the ECHR—ultimately, EasyBusiness received a groundswell of more than 500 landowner applications appealing to the court, resulting in a collective suit. ECHR became a third party to provide expert economic and legislative background. Overall, these efforts unlocked a range of new opportunities and created a feasible balance of powers.

On Coalitions

Transformative policy change can't happen without allies. Unfortunately, at the outset, it was difficult for EasyBusiness to find partners who fully supported the free-market farmland model for Ukraine. They were fortunate, however, to find partners who supported the general idea of opening up the sale of farmland in Ukraine.

"Only later did we promote our idea of an open farmland market among all our partners," said Andrew Shpakov, CEO of EasyBusiness. "This approach helps to consolidate as many partners to ultimately help with advocacy of the reform."

EasyBusiness was also fortunate to have fellow Atlas Network experts to turn to for this fight, and it was able to tap partners that included the Centre for Economic Strategy, Ekonomichna Pravda, Ukrainian Economic Freedoms Foundation, and others for help in spreading the word. These partners were able to lend another credible voice to the cause of land reform by taking part in the public submission of a complaint to the Constitutional Court of Ukraine claiming that the moratorium is illegal, among other major lifts.

On Storytelling

For EasyBusiness, this campaign required not only the support and partnership of other research and advocacy organizations but also help from landowners themselves.

Because it wasn't clear to many people how Ukraine's land sales restrictions were affecting them, EasyBusiness shared the stories of those affected to create momentum behind the cause of reform.

The group's farmland.in.ua online portal helped identify landowners who wanted to join the fight.

Sofia Zelenchuk and Viktor Tsytsyura were two of those landowners, and after using EasyBusiness' online portal to appeal to the ECHR, they ultimately became the two plaintiffs in the case against the Ukrainian government—and won.

EasyBusiness told the story of 79-year-old Viktor, who received his property certificates from the government in 2008. In his old age, Viktor can no longer work the land and would prefer to sell it so he can retire comfortably. Ukraine's ban on farmland sale forced him to stay on property he couldn't afford. By elevating Viktor's story, EasyBusiness showed the public the victims of bad land policy.

They also provided an avenue for Viktor to become an active participant in the reform movement—he attended the group's public educational events and communicated frequently with EasyBusiness team members over the phone during the fight. Viktor even came to Kyiv to participate in a panel discussion with politicians, activists, and experts. EasyBusiness' video featuring Viktor's story was viewed more than 100,000 times on social media.

Without EasyBusiness' efforts in Ukraine, the country's landowners would still have no hope of overturning the restrictions that prevent them from freely buying and selling farmland.

Discussion Questions

- Are there laws in your country that prevent free exercise of property rights? What are they and who are the people who are affected most?
- Does your think tank participate in taking legal action against the government? Why or why not? Are there coalition allies who could be helpful to you in this way?
- How can you go about finding people whose lives would benefit from the reforms you advocate? How can you tell their stories effectively?
- How can you make the case that property rights are just as important as civil and human rights when it comes to protecting yourself and your livelihood from government restrictions and abuse?

Note

1. IJ defines a win as a favorable court ruling, a favorable settlement, or a legislative reform in response to a lawsuit.

SECTION IV
Case Studies on Business and Occupational Licensing

The ability to participate in the formal market is key to prosperity. Formal market participation provides formal institutional protections. When you operate in a formal market, for example, disputes are more likely to be handled peaceably in court. Access to credit and other financial instruments increases considerably. Planning for the future is more feasible when trust and institutions provide stability and predictability.

Unfortunately, in many places, the barriers to join the formal market are unacceptably high. Not only do expensive government licensing fees prevent very modest businesses from registering, they also introduce opportunities for corrupt bureaucrats to solicit bribes, thus increasing the cost of entering the legal market. Furthermore, in many places. the number of government agencies required to approve a license introduces confusion and delays, which have real costs that are often too much to ask of very low-income entrepreneurs. Special interests can often use licensing to prevent competition, providing protections for the well established at the expense of low-income entrants. Only when we eliminate or simplify those barriers will talented, low-income populations have a real chance to achieve prosperity.

Versions of the case studies in this section are available at AtlasNetwork.org.

Opening Up Legal Markets to Low-Income Populations

Centre for Development and Enterprises
Great Lakes, Burundi

Introduction

Burundi is among the lowest-ranked countries in the World Bank's flagship *Doing Business* report, which ranks nations based on the ease of doing business. Political volatility and a corrupt, extremely centralized government has created a difficult economic environment for anyone not affiliated or loyal to the ruling class.

The Centre for Development Enterprises Great Lakes, or CDE–Great Lakes, fights to reduce the obstacles to prosperity and opportunity market in Burundi, Rwanda, and the Democratic Republic of Congo based on the principles of a free society and the free market.

Specifically, the Centre for Development Enterprises Great Lakes fought to dramatically reduce the licensing costs to become a legitimate business, which had been an insurmountable barrier to many would-be business owners. The group has also created programs to train and educate the country's next generation of entrepreneurs, which will help stimulate Burundi's economy and lift up its people.

To achieve this, CDE–Great Lakes launched its Birashoboka Project. The term "birashoboka" is a local Kirundi word from Burundi that means "it's possible." Through this project, CDE–Great Lakes is training the next generation of Burundian social entrepreneurs and fighting to make the country's laws and economic climate fairer and riper for their success.

79

Here's how CDE–Great Lakes changed the landscape for business development in Burundi:

- CDE–Great Lakes' work successfully led to the Burundi government cutting the cost of a business license to a fourth of its initial price, from US$78 to US$22 (140,000 francs to 40,000 francs, Burundian currency).
- CDE–Great Lakes has trained and educated more than 1,500 entrepreneurs on the specific challenges they face, giving them the knowledge they need to successfully navigate their new business ventures.
- The people of Burundi believe reform is possible and have been inspired to kickstart the next wave of entrepreneurship in their country.

CDE–Great Lakes' story offers lessons on how to:

- Lead by example, giving people faith that change can happen in their own lives
- Bring together all key stakeholders to educate all parties on the merits of a policy change
- Overcome fears of speaking out in the face of authoritarianism by leading with research and a strong media campaign, then following up with coalition building.

Project Narrative

In many African countries, including Burundi, there is little to no economic competition because the only businesses that exist do so with the blessing of a corrupt government.

These businesses bribe officials and maintain market power, resulting in high prices that cause consumers to suffer and a marketplace that locks out most citizens. Large monopolies have no incentive to innovate, so wages stay low and big business owners share huge profits with their government allies.

On the other hand, in countries where the market is open and the rule of law enforced, business dynamism increases, and people from other countries begin flocking to those regions. This was true for South Africa when it was thriving—people from all over sub-Saharan Africa went to South Africa to work, shop, and go to university.

Burundi is both one of the world's poorest and most corrupt countries. A turbulent and over-reaching government makes life unpredictable and upward mobility challenging. Perhaps in Burundi more than anywhere else in the world, people need the free market to give them hope of a better future.

Burundians needed to know a better future is possible, and that need for a feeling of hope and possibility is why CDE–Great Lakes launched its Birashoboka Project. CDE–Great Lakes' challenge was to accomplish these reforms in a country with a repressive authoritarian government.

Birashoboka is laid out in two parts. The first involves selecting, training, and assisting potential entrepreneurs in good business practices so that their businesses are able to thrive within their communities. The second involves strategic reforms aimed at improving scores on the *Doing Business* report, on which Burundi is currently ranked 186 out of 190. This poor ranking is due to the rigorous 10-step process that is required to start a business. As a result, many would-be entrepreneurs move to the informal economy. The Birashoboka project also seeks to change banking practices in order to ease the process of opening accounts.

CDE–Great Lakes has driven several important reforms that make business registration more accessible in Burundi. The fee to register a business has been slashed from about US$78 to US$22 in a country whose GDP per capita was roughly US$320 in 2017. The time it takes to register a business has been reduced from months to just one day. Banks had previously been required by law to charge interest rates of 18 percent for business loans and to impose a fee of US$16 to open business bank accounts, but thanks to the Birashoboka campaign, the interest rates have been reduced to 10 percent, and the required fees have been removed completely.

The impacts these reforms have had in a short time is already evident. From 2017 to 2018, the number of new business registrations increased 49.84 percent. In 2017, the number of new registrants increased only 5.34 percent.

Key Insights

On Navigating Difficult Political Environments

In Burundi, a strong authoritarian government presented a significant barrier to reform. That's why in addition to working directly with the people of Burundi on its Birashaboka campaign, CDE–Great Lakes talked to insiders to help them understand why these economic improvements were working toward the same end officials were seeking—a strong Burundian economy.

"We faced threats from members of the government because of the misunderstanding of the causes of poverty in Burundi," said Aimable Manirakiza, founder and CEO of CDE–Great Lakes.

Officials in Burundi are afraid of the exploitation of data in public because they fear the data will be used to propel real reports likely to distort reality or to tarnish the country's image. Fortunately, CDE–Great Lakes identified public servants who were willing to participate in face-to-face discussions and who responded favorably to the organization's research.

To take advantage of these face-to-face meetings, the CDE–Great Lakes team devised two key messages that showed officials how more business freedom and a reduced cost of doing business were not only the moral choice but also the expedient choice for the government.

The first argument showed parliamentarians that their economic restrictions deterred business investment from coming into the country. CDE–Great Lakes' research and data showed that harsh limitations on economic growth kept businesses from locating or relocating in Burundi. The group explained the importance of a welcoming economy, which helped officials understand that more

82

freedom would translate to more business investment and thus a more prosperous economy.

CDE–Great Lakes' second argument built on the first—that by creating an "informal sector" through restrictive fees and regulations, the government foregoes a significant tax base. The think tank was able to show that by reducing fees and barriers, the Burundian government would actually see an increase in tax revenue.

On Coalitions

Fighting for a better future means risking death in countries where oppressive rulers reign. Burundi has had a turbulent history, even after gaining independence from Belgium in the 1960s. After just 100 days in office, the country's first democratically elected president was assassinated in 1993. The country's current president overlooked Burundi's two-term constitutional limit and claimed a third term in 2015. This drastic step incited violent outbursts during which hundreds of Burundians were killed. Time and again, the Burundi government uses violence and intimidation to silence dissenters.

CDE–Great Lakes leaders knew it would be easier to take on this reform fight if they weren't standing alone. They worked hard to develop a sweeping network of groups pushing for the government to lift business restrictions. They fostered relationships with grassroots bloggers online and persuaded influencers and groups with big microphones, including people within government when possible, to vocally support their cause. Essentially, Manirakiza and his team believed that the more voices you can include in your movement, the stronger you'll be.

"In the face of an authoritarian regime, it is very important to think big about limiting the oppression of such a government as that of Burundi," Manirakiza said. "We were fortunate to also draw the attention of some civil society leaders and opposition members of the Burundian Parliament to support the cause of our campaign. The different groups have been useful in launching the Birashoboka campaign with measurable effects so far."

On Creating Hope

When people have endured decades of political instability and poverty, it's hard to imagine a world where freedom and prosperity thrive. They need help seeing the possibility of a better future. They need a standard bearer to light the way.

CDE–Great Lakes knew that hope could be kindled because the people of Burundi harbor a strong desire to work and prosper. Many Burundians' entrepreneurial spirit lay dormant, as they believed building a business of their own was impossible.

Burundians are entrepreneurs by nature—it's in their blood.

For a long time, entrepreneurship was synonymous with self-employment because of weak job prospects. CDE–Great Lakes is stoking the fires of the country's innate desire for entrepreneurship with this innovative new campaign. The Birashoboka campaign's main goal, in addition to drastically decreasing the cost of starting a business and giving people the tools they need to achieve success, was to harness and unleash that latent drive.

"More important than these efforts was the hope we gave them," Manirakiza said. "We worked tirelessly and believed we could change the system."

On Achieving Impact

Possibility is turning into reality in Burundi because of CDE–Great Lakes' Birashoboka campaign.

Thanks to the group's efforts, more than 1,500 entrepreneurs have been educated on the specific challenges they face. The Ministry of Commerce has eased the burden of registering businesses by reducing the startup cost from 140,000 francs (US$78) to 40,000 francs (US$22). Also, banks have sought ways to better serve their clients by streamlining the process and allowing people to set up accounts over the phone, as well as developing unique accounts for entrepreneurs.

Thanks to CDE–Great Lakes's efforts, it's now easier for entrepreneurs to start a business and positively contribute to their communities.

Discussion Questions

- What does it take to register a business in your country? Are there ways to simplify the process and make it more affordable especially for low-income registrants?
- How can you present your research and recommendations in a way that would appeal to a variety of politicians? Are there practical benefits you can focus on?
- How can you make the most of a small operating budget? Can you get creative about optimizing in-kind resources, volunteer support, or cultivating nontraditional donors?

Economic Opportunity After Prison

Georgia Center for Opportunity, United States

Introduction

The state of Georgia leads the United States in the per capita number of people under correctional supervision. Approximately one in every 13 Georgians is currently incarcerated. In order to tackle this crisis head on, the Georgia Center for Opportunity (GCO), through its Prisoner Reentry Initiative, implemented the following steps to change public policy in Georgia:

1. Interviewed and recruited knowledgeable experts in the field of criminal justice to join the organization's newly developed Working Group
2. Over the course of a year, met with the Working Group to develop policy solutions that are apolitical, draw wide support, and have the greatest chance of creating major changes in criminal reentry
3. Wrote and distributed two landmark reports
4. Met with legislators and the Council on Criminal Justice Reform to ensure that proposed solutions were adopted quickly.

Because of the team's tireless work and the success of this program, GCO was one of the six finalists for the 2017 Templeton Freedom Award.

GCO is an independent and nonpartisan think tank located in Atlanta, Georgia. The organization is dedicated to researching and developing community-based policy solutions that create opportunities for low-income earners who are tethered to government programs that rob them of their humanity and hope. The team at

GCO promotes those solutions to policymakers and the public and helps innovative social enterprises deliver results on the ground. GCO shapes public policy and creates local community efforts that lead to a quality education, stable employment, and a healthy family life for a greater number of people in Georgia. It is focused on breaking the barriers to social mobility in the state by helping individual citizens and their communities flourish.

Between 1990 and 2011, the state of Georgia's prison population more than doubled to nearly 56,000 inmates. State spending on corrections soared as well, from $492 million to more than $1 billion annually. Despite this substantial investment, Georgia's recidivism rate (the number of individuals who return to prison within three years of their release) remained virtually unchanged for close to a decade.

In 2009, the Pew Center on the States released a study showing that Georgia led the country in the number of adults under some form of correctional supervision, one in 13. Nationwide, that number is 1 in 31. When these individuals are released, most are not prepared for success outside the prison walls. Nationally, nearly 65 percent of former inmates will be rearrested and, in Georgia, about 30 percent will find themselves back in prison within three years.

Studies show that in order to achieve a successful transition back into society, returning citizens need steady employment, safe and affordable housing, and reliable transportation. Ironically, these fundamental needs are the most challenging for them to secure.

Employment, housing, and transportation are largely interrelated, as it is hard to have one without the other. For instance, it is difficult for a person to keep a job without having a place to live relatively nearby; it is doubtful a person can continue to pay rent without having a regular source of income; and it is challenging to find housing or commute to work without a reliable means of transportation. This Catch-22 is what makes reentry so intimidating for many getting out of prison.

However, if those three major needs are met, the chance that former inmates will end up back behind bars is greatly reduced.

To address these challenges, in 2011 the Georgia General Assembly created the Special Council on Criminal Justice Reform. Two years later, the council conducted a review of Georgia's reentry services and found that while a good deal of work was underway, the statewide effort suffered from balkanization and numerous barriers to success.

Because of these findings, the council developed the Georgia Prisoner Reentry Initiative, which laid the foundation for a five-year effort expected to make Georgia a leader in recidivism reduction.

Project Narrative

Georgia's high recidivism rate is costly to the state's communities and families, to public safety, and to taxpayers. Knowing the state was committed to improving this area, GCO made it a priority to enhance public safety and control spending by helping prisoners reintegrate into society.

Following a conversation with a former Chief Justice of the Georgia Supreme Court, the team began speaking to prison wardens, prisoners, transition center leaders, and the heads of the State Board of Pardons and Paroles and the Reentry Services Division for the Georgia Department of Corrections.

In July 2013, after many months of research, nearly four dozen interviews, and visits to four of the state's prison facilities, the organization launched its Prisoner Reentry Working Group. The priority when building this group was gathering people with expertise in Georgia's correctional system and a strong interest in improving outcomes for prisoners returning to the community. The nine Working Group members were selected regardless of political affiliation; however, the majority of the group wound up being center-left.

Members agreed to meet at GCO's office in Atlanta once a month for a year while they developed policy and service-related solutions to improve prisoner reentry experiences, reduce recidivism, and improve positive outcomes for prisoners (such as job attainment and retention, housing stability, staying sober and drug-free, and meeting debt obligations). The Working Group would then present their recommendations to legislators, the governor, and the state's Council on Criminal Justice Reform.

During the group's first meeting, the members quickly decided upon several broad areas of focus for policy solutions. Those areas included:

- *Employment*: Removing barriers to entering the workplace and increasing opportunities for former prisoners to obtain and retain employment upon release.
- *Reentry Courts*: Creating courts that specialize in working with prisoners as they are reentering the community.
- *Transitional Centers*: Increasing the capacity of Georgia's transitional centers to serve more people and exploring whether centers specialized to work with specific kinds of offenders could be more effective in reducing recidivism.

While the scope of these topics is large, the Working Group zeroed in on specific, common-sense solutions that offered the greatest potential for measurable improvement.

With the guidance of the Working Group, GCO authored two reports: "Increasing Employment Opportunities for Ex-Offenders," published in December 2013, and "A High Price to Pay," released in December 2014. These reports focused on ways to improve workforce reentry for formerly incarcerated individuals as well as exploring solutions to minimize the role debt has in driving recidivism. The policy solutions in each report were promoted to policymakers, the media, and the general public and presented to the Georgia Council on Criminal Justice Reform in 2014.

GCO's Prisoner Reentry Initiative focuses on the rehabilitation and restoration of former offenders with their family and community. This program, which aims to help newly released individuals gain employment and reconnect with their loved ones, has been credited with positively impacting the state's justice system.

The Working Group's recommendations, which were compiled into two reports and presented to the Georgia Council on Criminal

Justice Reform, were incorporated in the Council's final report to the governor. Over the past several years, nearly all of the recommendations were passed into law and policy changes were implemented. These legislative and policy changes include:

Recommendations Implemented from the Report "Increasing Employment Opportunities for Ex-Offenders":

- Passed SB 365 in April 2014: Gives judges discretion to not automatically suspend driver's licenses for drug offenders who committed a non-driving-related offense, as well as protects employers from liability in hiring a person with a criminal record.
- Banned the Box in February 2015: Georgia became the first state in the South to officially "ban the box" through an executive order issued by Governor Nathan Deal. This effort removed the checkbox located on applications for state employment that compels the applicant to divulge any criminal record.
- Passed HB 328 in 2015: Allows offenders who have completed a drug court program to be eligible for obtaining professional licensing.

Recommendations Implemented from the Report "A High Price to Pay":

- The Division of Child Support Services, superior court judges, probation, and parole now communicate on how to best ensure people involved in the criminal justice system pay child support while receiving the necessary supervision and assistance they need to find a job and make consistent payments once in the community.
- Passed SB 367 in 2016: Made it easier for recently incarcerated individuals to obtain employment through greater access to occupational licensing; reinstated driver's licenses for those convicted of drug-related offenses that did not involve a motor vehicle; expanded funding for Parental Accountability Courts (see more information below) that reduce incarceration and

encourage parents to support their children; added liability protection for employers.

- March 2015: The Division of Child Support Services revised its policy concerning releasing suspended driver's licenses to those who are behind in child support payments in order to remove a barrier to work.

Expansion of Parental Accountability Courts

- Based in part on research conducted by GCO, Georgia expanded the state's system of Parental Accountability Courts from 10 to more than 30, with an additional 19 coming. This one reform will go a long way to helping get people to work who would otherwise be caught up in the justice system, while also helping more parents be a part of their children's lives.

The reforms recommended by GCO that are now state law and administrative policy will help tens of thousands of Georgians annually who are impacted by the correctional system to re-enter society, get back on their feet, and lead self-sufficient lives. This means more intact families, less crime, and fewer taxpayer dollars going to prisons.

The reforms spearheaded by GCO are driving positive trends, such as a 6 percent drop in Georgia's prison population since 2012—a $264 million saving for taxpayers—and a predicted 11-percent drop in recidivism.

Atlas Network's CEO, Brad Lips, praised GCO's innovative approach to criminal justice reform.

"GCO's Prisoner Reentry Initiative demonstrates that compassion for the incarcerated and their families can be aligned with the interests of taxpayers and public safety," Lips said. "It's a wonderful initiative that deserves to be emulated."

GCO's "Hiring Well, Doing Good" and "Georgia Works!" initiatives are two other programs that have spun out from the success of GCO's Prisoner Reentry project.

"Hiring Well, Doing Good" holds events that aim to develop new partnerships between businesses and those serving the unemployed so that more people find work.

The events also seek to inspire business leaders to expand opportunities to those who are struggling to find work by learning from their peers and understanding the extent of the problem. Topics at these events cover legal and liability considerations, tax incentives available to businesses hiring from certain populations, nonprofits with which businesses can partner, and the experiences of other businesses.

These events have garnered support from the Atlanta Falcons, Uber, Georgia-Pacific, the Arthur M. Blank Foundation, Goodwill Industries, and CKS Packaging. More than 125 community leaders attended GCO's "Hiring Well, Doing Good" event and roughly 30 businesses signed intentional efforts to hire the chronically underemployed.

The purpose of Georgia Works! is to develop and implement cost-effective, comprehensive programs that meet the needs of a diverse population working to break the cycles of homelessness, addiction, and criminal recidivism.

The program houses participants at their facility for one year, during which time they earn at least $7.40 an hour working 30 or more hours a week. The program is designed to break down the barriers that keep the unemployed in cycles of dependency by treating addictions, offering personal support and life preparation tools, and providing GED classes.

Georgia Works! also helps participants meet the necessities of a normal life, such as getting a driver's license and setting up a bank account.

Key Insights

On Coalitions

Randy Hicks, GCO's president and CEO, credits much of the project's success to the strategic partnerships they developed across the state. "These partnerships," he said while speaking at Atlas Network's Liberty Forum & Freedom Dinner in New York City, "had an exponential effect because they allowed us to look much larger than we were. In the end, we had a de facto coalition that made sure all those recommendations passed when it came to removing barriers to employment. They were so passionate and ready to go to work for it."

- Finding the right partnerships to amplify your policy solutions is essential for smaller organizations and projects with tighter budgets.

On Diverse Stakeholders

By developing the Working Group, GCO was able to bring together diverse stakeholders to address recidivism in Georgia. This model, which was vital to its success, provided an effective strategy for bridging research, policy, and practice in order to achieve real reform. Hicks stated, "As we did a sweep through the state [to find members for the Working Group], we were looking for the people who knew the most. We didn't need to be ideologically aligned. We just needed to know what they knew, so we took the time to seek them out and listen to their concerns and experiences. This way we had the clearest possible understanding of what was going on in the state when it came to prisoner recidivism."

- Many of the Working Group members disagreed with GCO on the organization's other policy issues, but they were still willing to work together to achieve marketable solutions to the problem of large prison populations and high recidivism rates.
- Working Group members were a passionate cadre of influential leaders ready to advocate for and defend their recommended policy solutions.

On Thinking Outside the Box

As a nonpartisan think tank, GCO encouraged members of the Working Group to think boldly when considering the possible solutions to reduce recidivism in Georgia. In contrast to government commissions and other similar bodies, independent think tanks like GCO are afforded greater freedom to champion ideas that may push the envelopes of conventional wisdom or current political feasibility.

- Allowing your organization to think boldly creates an opportunity to discover policy solutions that have not yet been explored, or ones that other organizations have thought were unfeasible.

On Balancing Different Viewpoints

As the project was just beginning, a Working Group member advocated for a policy that would have put limits on or instituted a quota system for the racial makeup of those arrested and charged for crimes. The group understood this was a politically unworkable approach and wouldn't lead to policy change.

- When developing a group like GCO's Prisoner Reentry Working Group, it is vital to communicate the goals of the group upfront. Knowing that this policy recommendation would not be adopted, and thus would not help the group achieve their goals, the idea was subsequently tabled.
- During the Working Group's monthly meetings, GCO made sure the group stayed away from buzzwords and fringe issues surrounding prisoner reentry and remained focused on what needed to be dealt with to create change in the state.

On Political Tradeoffs

GCO received some pushback from legislative leaders and the governor, who didn't want to adopt some of Working Group's reform ideas. Georgia was in a budget deficit, and ideas like the state bonding program and tax credits for hiring ex-convicts would cost the state money. But due to the fact that GCO sought out strategic partnerships and built its Working Group from the state's foremost experts on criminal justice reform, total pushback on policy solutions was minimal.

After forming a Working Group on the issue in 2013, GCO produced expert insights in two landmark reports. In the years that followed, nearly all the organization's recommendations were adopted into law, helping to broaden opportunities for former inmates reintegrating into society.

Discussion Questions

- Think about your policy priorities in your country. What injustices do your reforms correct for? Who will benefit as a result?
- How clear are you internally about your ultimate goals? Are you thinking big about change? What milestones in the next 12–18 months would demonstrate you are on track?
- How can you build alliances with others and work together toward change?

Achieving Inclusive Prosperity

Centre for Civil Society, India

Introduction

India is a country in transition. Vaulted to the global stage due to globalization, its GDP has tripled since 2000, following economic liberalization in 1991. In 2001, it was branded as one of the BRICS (Brazil, Russia, India, China, South Africa) economies, highlighting its growing economic position. While bringing up the rear in per capita GDP among its BRICS peers—including Brazil, Russia, China, and South Africa—the IMF estimates that India's GDP will grow between 7 and 8 percent over the next few years, faster than all of them.

As the country aims to prove its nimbleness in persisting as a top tier economy, civil society in the populous nation is facing its own growing pains. Often cited as the world's largest democracy, over 800 million of India's 1.3 billion people are eligible to vote. And they do, with over 65-percent voter participation in the 2014 general election. The right to vote, however, does not automatically result in representative government or the protection of personal freedoms. In fact, social issues have emerged that threaten to split the diverse nation at the seams.

In some ways stuck in a time capsule, India struggles with a lingering caste system and a residual socialist framework from its colonial past, including its elaborate system of bureaucracy referred to as "License Raj." Extreme poverty, illiteracy, and other social ills plague hundreds of millions, often preserved by archaic regulations that inhibit progress from the bottom up. The country is teeming with diverse people and innovative ideas, but for India to maintain the momentum it has achieved, it needs constructive reform that permeates the country.

Enter the Centre for Civil Society, India's leading and globally recognized think tank, which aims to advance social change through public policy, often targeting change at the lowest levels of the social ladder.

Celebrating its 20th anniversary in 2017, the Centre for Civil Society is regularly ranked among the best public policy research organizations in the world by the University of Pennsylvania's Think Tanks and Civil Society Program. Focusing on education, livelihood, business climate, and policy training, CCS strives to put ideas into action. Parth Shah, the center's founder and president, is keen to clarify that CCS "is more than a think tank; it's a do tank."

While pursuing a doctorate in economics in the United States, Shah first encountered the notion that a society hallmarked by freedom leads to personal enrichment as well as economic and social progress. That idea led him to connect with several think tanks in the 1990s. Not long after he began his academic career as a professor of economics at the University of Michigan, he started to crave a more active role in ameliorating social problems. He returned to his home country of India and launched CCS, where he continues to guide its focus on evidence-based research.

CCS is committed to affecting change through policy impact, based on the belief that direct action only addresses symptoms, while focusing on policy change targets the root of social issues. That vision resonates with the team of well-trained professionals who partner with Shah to make it happen.

Bhakti Patil, a researcher and CCS' development manager, explains that approximately 35 staff members are organized into three categories: research; advocacy, which includes engaging media, policymakers, and Hindi language initiatives; and CCS Academy, which targets students, media, and policymakers with specialized training in the political process and the need for ethical and data-driven policy solutions.

Even so, well-trained team members and good operating strategy and practices do not ensure success. Patil explains that there is a strong prejudice in society that "markets are for the rich and leave behind the poor." To change hearts and minds, CCS has developed a deep infrastructure of contacts and consistently provides them with quality research. Over time, this approach has built credibility and provides key opportunities to influence policy.

Access is only part of the obstacle, says Shah, because when political will does turn toward market reforms, "government prefers to use cronyism, regulations, and subsidies to spur the private sector." This adds its own layer of challenges to CCS' work, but the team has not shied away from addressing these factors head on.

The team concentrates on bottom-of-the-pyramid reforms affecting the lowest rung of the social ladder. This assuages social bias against markets while demonstrating their power to dramatically improve the lives of the poor and, in turn, the country's growth.

Project Narrative

CCS has participated in various Atlas Network trainings and programs over many years, which Shah believes have helped the organization grow. With the Leveraging Indices for Free Enterprise (LIFE) Program, CCS leadership saw a unique opportunity to further expand their program portfolio. In many ways, in fact, the program looked tailor-made for the environment CCS faced in India.

The timing of the launch of LIFE was ideal, notes Shah, because the government that was elected in 2014 had just begun talking about India's floundering ranking on the World Bank's *Doing Business* report. This provided CCS with a remarkable opportunity to harness the political winds to carry its ideas to greater influence.

As an established institution, CCS has developed procedures for conducting public policy work, honed to the political and cultural context of its environment. When setting a game plan for LIFE, however, the team had to revise some of its tactics. For instance, CCS has often worked on business reform initiatives, but such efforts have been a bit piecemeal because they generally fall outside their core areas of education and livelihood. "LIFE integrated this work under one umbrella," remarks Patil. "It helped us to improve our strategy."

Although LIFE was a new way for CCS to consider its work, its efforts were guided by established procedures. First, it focused on finding key problems that were ripe for change. Second, the team identified what factors impact those issues, ranging from the regulations that supported them to the key staff with knowledge to draft reforms. Third, it built research and analysis in the targeted areas. And fourth, the communications group constructed an advocacy plan around the research.

Carrying out its plan, the research team explored the areas where India was ranked particularly low to help set the specific project targets. Then they cross-referenced those areas with their internal capabilities, identifying who had the core competencies to address the subject matter. They looked specifically at who in their organization had worked in related policy areas, and broadly at who had skills that could be transferable to the new areas of concentration. The resultant focus areas included various subtargets under the larger categories of the requirements of starting a business and the time to enforce contracts.

The team produced 14 research papers on the specific topics, ranging from an eight-point action plan on creating a framework for contract enforcement to an international analysis of how to penalize people whose checks bounce. The papers were all packaged with multipronged advocacy plans to target both central and state governments. "We also heavily engaged the media," notes Patil, adding that the content was also integrated into their policy trainings.

Starting a Business (*Doing Business*, World Bank)

- Reduce the number of procedures from 11 to 9 (Delhi) and 13 to 10 (Mumbai).
- Reduce the number of days from 27 to 22 (Delhi) and from 30 to 25 (Mumbai).
- Reduce the paid-in minimum capital requirement to zero via repeal. As of 2015, the requirement was 111.2 percent.

Enforcing Contracts

- Reduce the number of days from 1,420 to 500 days.

As the project progressed, CCS integrated an additional goal of persuading the government to enforce the 2014 Street Vendors Act. While seemingly outside the scope of the selected index, the effort was identified as a proxy for the other targets.

Having previously worked on the structural barriers to education by analyzing the steps needed to deregulate the process of starting schools, CCS concluded it could focus the same skills toward identifying the hurdles to starting a business and develop viable policy solutions. Drawing on their past efforts to formalize street vendors as businesses, CCS decided to also focus on further establishing those popular jobs as a recognized sector of the economy.

A unique feature of their approach that has garnered credibility from society at large is their use of pilot programs to test proposed policy ideas. CCS had previously succeeded in legally legitimizing street vendors as businesses, seen in the passage of the Street Vendors Act in 2014. However, some states have refused to implement the Act, citing federalist discretion, thus delaying the benefits of legitimacy for millions in the street vendor sector. As an initiative of their LIFE project, CCS lawyers took the case to court, winning a judgment that mandates states to follow the central court's decision.

In a related initiative, CCS pursued and succeeded in another legal challenge to classify bamboo as a grass rather than a tree. While seemingly benign, the change dramatically impacts commerce, especially for the poor, because trees are protected from harvesting, selling, and trading across localities. Again, CCS's efforts resulted in real change that enhances the economic opportunities at the bottom of the pyramid while also moving the needle on broad indices.

This was a round-about way to target the resultant index scores, but that wasn't the main driver for the change. "When we started LIFE, we didn't focus on street vendors since it didn't directly apply to the index," says Patil. "But we decided mid-project to integrate street (and bamboo) vendor work back in because shifting the index is not our end goal. We are pursuing a larger scale vision of improving the business climate for the long term."

Furthermore, the decision to focus on bottom-of-the-pyramid industries served a secondary purpose because it helped to carry CCS' policy advocacy into the mainstream. In India, street vendors are ubiquitous, and most people see them every day. CCS' policy advocacy on the topic can therefore be understood by a broader audience than much of their other work.

Complementary to building social capital at the bottom of the social pyramid, CCS targeted policymakers and heads of ministries with their research and reports, relying on their own persistence and the policymakers' self-interest to drive further success. When asked how CCS first established connections in the government, Shah simply says, "Lots of lunches," expounding that gaining access involved lots of knocking on doors and conversations before CCS became a recognized voice. The CCS staff continues to foster relationships with officials, sending updates on new research studies, advising on emergent issues, and meeting ministry members to share insights. These connections don't always result in favorable results, but CCS' consistency has proffered deep credibility.

The persistence of this outreach, matched with the quality of research produced, has resulted in invitations to help form policy. As the government has sought to advance India's ranking in the *Doing Business* report, various officials solicited CCS for input. Through the course of outreach for the LIFE initiatives, CCS presented its research before the Rajya Sabha (the upper house of Parliament), resulting in several recommendations being endorsed by the panel. They also presented their judicial reform proposals before the Indian Law Commission, arguing for expediting the process of litigation for contract enforcement.

A long list of outdated and obsolete laws still on the books yet only enforced arbitrarily was the main factor contributing to India's low score on the *Doing Business* report. CCS decided to package these disparate laws into a unified initiative to repeal them and developed a campaign under the LIFE banner labeled "Repeal 100 Laws." So far, 23 of them have been repealed, followed by a state-specific effort in Maharashtra, where 19 of 25 proposed laws were repealed.

Beyond this remarkable success, the initiative created momentum that led the government itself to repeal 1,200 redundant laws, with 1,800 more identified to be scrapped. CCS also launched a social media campaign to call attention to bad laws, using the hashtag "#LawsWithFlaws" to engage the public in the process of finding laws that ought to go. Pairing this outreach with a monthly session of interactive discussion on Twitter, they have reached more than 15,000 unique users.

The success of the legal campaigns and public engagement led CCS to further innovate. Despite being a fairly large organization, CCS realized its own limitations in maintaining momentum in all the areas of its LIFE project. They brought in additional interns to support their data collection and also reached out to think tanks and social engagement organizations already active in legal research and outreach to help drive their projects' success. "Moving to a more collaborative framework and getting boots on the ground were new features of our action," says Patil. "The LIFE program more or less opened our eyes to collaboration. It wasn't something totally new, but it became a much larger component."

By working with organizations with existing competencies in areas new to CCS, the team could be confident that progress would continue while being able to pivot its own resources back to their comparative advantages, namely research and high-level advocacy.

As India stands with one foot in the past and one in the future, the country faces tensions regarding policy reform. For instance, the climate of cronyism runs deep due to the country's history with the License Raj system that fueled India's attempts at industrial policy for almost half of the 20th century. "Predictably and understandably," states Shah regarding the over-regulated environment, "people take short cuts and use the state to stop competitors," exacerbating India's struggle with rampant corruption. This has further prejudiced the country against market-oriented pursuits. The onset of globalization has begun to wear down this prejudice, however, as people experience the transformative power of aviation, telecommunications, and banking, although progress can be slow.

Elements of the country's caste system also show up in policy discussions. Some claim that markets are for the rich and harm the poor, but as Shah recounts, "when you start advocating for granting more power to the poor, the same people who complain about how markets deprive the poor, they say the poor are not capable of making those decisions." Addressing this cognitive dissonance requires patience.

These attributes of Indian society have hampered CCS' LIFE project, but the challenges CCS faces often double as opportunities if addressed appropriately. By identifying ways to align the interests of their detractors with reform, usually by demonstrating that their own lives would improve, progress can be made, albeit slowly. Fortunately, patience has been a trait CCS has been forced to develop since its founding.

India has been moving up the rankings in the *Ease of Doing Business Index* since CCS started the LIFE project. The government has eliminated the minimum capital requirements for starting a business, the time needed to enforce contracts has decreased by nearly 65 percent, and the procedures and days needed to start a business have been reduced. While difficult to causally link CCS' efforts with these successes, the evidence is pretty convincing.

CCS' direct engagement with policymakers, which provided a solid foundation on which they built the LIFE project, has also born fruit. The Department of Industrial Policy and Promotion has adopted several CCS recommendations for improving India's business climate, and its proposal for an online business registry has also been implemented. These are just some of the successes CCS achieved throughout the program, and it looks like the momentum will continue.

While India's *Doing Business* score is based on rules and regulations only New Delhi and Mumbai, which acts as a constraint on their efforts under the LIFE project, Patil notes that moving forward, they plan to expand their work to more cities, implementing many of the same successful initiatives. They won't measure success based on the World Bank's index, but it will serve as a barometer.

Furthermore, they have begun a grassroots campaign to launch a "Repeal of Laws Day" on the country's Constitution Day, which is celebrated in late November, drawing on the success of previous business reforms to rally citizens and politicians to continue those efforts.

Key Insights

CCS has proven to be a formidable challenger to those trying to keep India stuck in its stagnant socialist past. Progress has been slow, but steady. To gain influence, the organization has had to develop robust capabilities not just in research and messaging but in connecting with disinterested or even hostile audiences, ranging from politicians to the public. In a country of over 1.3 billion people, that can result in a lot of voices to pacify. Many would see this as an insurmountable obstacle, but Parth Shah and his team at CCS have seen this as a challenge and have risen to meet it with a strong capacity for responsiveness and ability to adapt.

On Playing the Long Game

CCS has demonstrated great patience in building a strong reputation as a qualified voice on a host of public policy issues. Relationships take time, an important resource to nonprofits, because organizations are dependent on research and fundraising for short-term survival. Building a reliable and influential network, however, is instrumental in affecting structural policy change. CCS staff spent countless hours contacting, visiting, and educating policymakers and business leaders. This has come at the cost of other pursuits, but it is a long-term plan and has resulted in what both Shah and Patil credit as their greatest asset: credibility.

The team decided to pursue the added goal of street vendor reform, for example, even though it was not explicitly linked to one of the *Doing Business* categories. A result of those efforts is the expanded freedom of millions of entrepreneurs, which will undoubtedly influence the country's performance in formal index scores and rankings. The outcome was not known in advance, however, which reflects a fundamental resolve to trust principled convictions in pursuing the alleviation of poverty and hardship.

On Creating a Shared Vision

Human capital is at the core of CCS' success. Taking advantage of the strong labor market in India, CCS has combined distinct competencies to build a team capable of affecting change across a span of policy issues, drawing on diverse skills in concert to complement one another.

Its researchers' insights led to successful ventures into making real progress on improving scores on large *Doing Business* categories by focusing on details and effectively building the intellectual case for reform, including moving the country toward e-filing for businesses and certain legal issues. The legal team's tact in building and arguing cases led to expanded freedom for bottom-of-the-pyramid entrepreneurs and the broad scale repeal of antiquated and arbitrary laws. Even the board of directors is credited for advancing CCS' mission, according to Shah, because they hold respected positions in business, academia, and government, and further bolster CCS' credibility.

On Motivation for Success

CCS was founded to materially improve people's lives through improving access to free markets. CCS president Parth Shah, sums up the approach, "We are an idea-driven organization." This provides exceptional flexibility to transition the team's capabilities to a variety of topics and to undertake innovative approaches and not be beholden to specific policy issues. CCS has put policy ideas into action via pilot programs to demonstrate that its ideas work and has handed off successful programs to other organizations better equipped to handle particular issues. It has been willing to risk short-term success in order to pursue long-term structural policy changes.

Discussion Questions

- Has your organization ever been blinded by success? Are there initiatives or projects you have started that have gained traction but require your staff to spend time on things outside their realm of expertise? How could your organization hand these projects over to other organizations more equipped to keep them going in the long term?
- What specific elements of your country's history make advancing market-oriented reform difficult? How might you be able to turn that challenge into an opportunity?
- How difficult is it for an organization to reformat a major project midstream? What kind of risk tolerance does that require? CCS decided to integrate advocacy for street vendor reforms into their LIFE project, even though that was not directly tied to their target metrics. What do you think was at the root of their decision? Would your organization act similarly?
- The LIFE project prompted CCS to build capabilities in a policy area where it had previously not focused systematically. What could prompt your organization to pivot in a new direction? How would you decide whether or not to dedicate limited resources to such an initiative?
- Governing administrations change and political parties evolve. How can you pursue structural reforms that will last regardless of the shifts in political tide? Do your organization's current programs tend to be focuses on short- or long-term policy wins?

SECTION V
Case Studies on Privatization

Governments can be important actors in securing property rights, enforcing contracts, and settling disputes fairly and predictably. Because those functions are so important, they should be the focus of any efforts to improve government capability. By refocusing governments on core functions, we can anticipate improved institutions. We can also eliminate or minimize the distorting and debilitating effects of government involvement in noncore functions. In too many cases, government attempts to provide various goods and services have ended in dismal failure, characterized by exorbitant costs and low quality.

In some cases, the perverse result of this is that private providers are crowded out of the marketplace, leaving consumers with only government options. In other cases, private providers are expressly prohibited from competing, which is no recipe for discovering economic solutions that contribute to shared prosperity. We want competent, capable governments that defy corrupting influences. We are more likely to achieve that objective if we limit the scope of government to only those functions that are truly needed for a free and peaceful society to thrive.

Versions of the case studies in this section are available at AtlasNetwork.org.

Expanding Access to Reliable Electricity

Lebanese Institute for Market Studies, Lebanon

Introduction

Lebanon has been plagued by hours-long power outages since the 1970s. The government is the monopoly supplier of power, stifling innovation and competition that would have led to better electricity service for consumers. Thanks to the Lebanese Institute for Market Studies, however, the power market is now open to private competition, and the people of Lebanon can look forward to less government waste and overspending—and more light.

The Lebanese Institute for Market Studies, or LIMS, was founded in 2015 during one of the country's darkest moments since independence. The freedoms Lebanon's founding fathers had fought for began to erode as the government grew too large and reduced liberties. By 2015, public debt had reached 148 percent of GDP—so a team of Lebanese visionaries stepped up and created an organization that would work to restore economic freedom in Lebanon.

The team at LIMS works to empower the people of Lebanon and fight for their liberties using research, education, and thought-provoking discussions with public officials, the media, and the people.

Imagine living in a country where it's possible you might get cut off from running water, get stuck in your office elevator for hours, or have your life support stop functioning because you lack access to an adequate power supply. Now imagine that problem exists because the government you're required to fund is the monopoly supplier of power.

It's a maddening concept people in developed countries can't even fathom. But citizens of Lebanon understand this as their daily reality, as the average person experiences an average of 12 hours of rolling blackouts a day.

Government has proven it can't properly provide electricity to the people of Lebanon—but the free market, and the businesses and creative force it unleashes, can. Fortunately for the people of Lebanon, LIMS stepped in to fill the void of new ideas with original research and a fully-developed set of solutions that would open up the country's electricity market to private companies and lead to better power service for consumers.

Here's how LIMS changed the landscape for the Lebanese power market:

- LIMS drafted a blueprint for reform in 2014 that laid the ground-work for ending the Lebanese government's power monopoly. LIMS's vision was to cut government spending and to replace the public electricity monopoly with private competition.
- LIMS followed its research with a massive public awareness campaign. In 2016, LIMS did 33 television interviews on prime-time news and talk shows, 20 radio appearances, 42 newspaper interviews, and 50 online articles, all of which highlighted the group's push for change.
- Next, LIMS launched a persuasion campaign, holding 32 meet-ings with members of Parliament and ministers. LIMS officials laid out their plans and research, showing decisionmakers there was a better way to produce electricity in their country.
- On April 17, 2019, the Lebanese Parliament ratified a new elec-tricity plan that slashes subsidies to the state-run electricity company and clears the way for private companies to produce electricity.

Project Narrative

Electricity was introduced to Lebanon in 1906 when the Ottoman Empire allowed private Belgian investors to open the first electricity company in Beirut. It was then transferred to a

French company in 1923 and finally to the government in 1954. Since that date, the government has been the monopoly provider of electricity in Lebanon.

Blackouts started during the Lebanese civil war (1975–1990). After the war ended, peace came back to Lebanon. Electricity did not.

Since the Lebanese established monopoly control over the country's power, all attempts to solve the blackout crisis have centered on throwing more taxpayers dollars at the problem. It hasn't worked. The Lebanese government has spent $35 billion on electricity since 2010 without stopping the mass power outages that plague its people.

The lack of stable electricity goes far beyond a minor personal inconvenience. As Reuters writer Angus McDowell puts it, "Lebanon's electricity crisis has pushed it to the brink of financial ruin, as power cuts hobble the economy and subsidies have racked up one of the world's largest public debt burdens."

Lebanon spends over $1 billion a year on power subsidies, the equivalent of 40 percent of national debt. That's a big deal, considering that the country is spending half its budget on public debt. This massive and inefficient governmental spending, combined with the instability of the nation's power source and government, are a huge deterrent to business investment. Indeed, the country's economy has grown just 1–2 percent in recent years.

The challenge of getting anyone to act on this crisis was monumental. For starters, from 2014–2016, Lebanon was without a president. The problem has continued today, with a caretaker at the helm of government due to infighting by politicians.

Even though it's technically illegal to produce power privately, people in Lebanon have been turning to private generators for power. As of 2017, private generators offered service to 70 percent of households during blackouts.

"I am currently using cheap generators that are noisy, polluting, and not very efficient," said Abdullah, an entrepreneur who provides electricity during blackouts. "I would like to build more efficient power plants. I can handle all the logistics, and I already have a good client base. . . . Once it's legal, I would be able to borrow funds from the bank or attract investors to grow my business, which I cannot do right now."

Providers like Abdullah are responding to a market demand, but they are limited in what they can offer. Small-scale generators rely on pollutant-heavy fuels and are not a sustainable method of providing people with sufficient power.

To make meaningful changes to the dire situation facing the Lebanese people, LIMS created its "Turn the Lights On in Lebanon" advocacy campaign, aiming for a double reform: to cut electricity subsidies in Lebanon and to allow the private sector to enter the electricity production market. In order to achieve these two reforms, LIMS raised public awareness through a continuous presence in traditional and social media. The institute also reached out to political parties in order to obtain their support.

Breaking up a government monopoly is a gargantuan task—and it wasn't an easy or quick fight for LIMS. In 2014, the organization took the first step in its fight by drafting a policy proposition that became a blueprint for reform. LIMS's vision was to cut government spending and to replace the public electricity monopoly with private competition.

As a result of a major media and public awareness campaign in 2016, public opinion started moving from resigned pessimism to hopeful optimism now that LIMS had provided an alternative vision for how electricity could be produced.

LIMS leveraged changing public sentiment by applying pressure to legislators, holding meetings with members of Parliament and ministers privately and in the presence of their advisors. This was an important step because it persuaded government officials that the status quo wasn't working and gave them ideas for how to resolve the problem by embracing free-market principles.

While LIMS ramped up its behind-the-scenes conversations with Parliament and their public campaign, Lebanon continued suffering power outages. The Lebanese government planned to increase government-run power generation by building several new power plants and renting two additional "powerships," all at taxpayer expense. Powerships are ships that have been converted into a floating power plant and are responsible for 25 percent of Lebanese electricity output. LIMS decided enough was enough, stepping in to block this massive spending plan and promoting a market-oriented solution instead.

Any plan that simply props up the current system without serious reform is doomed to fail. LIMS knew the first step needed in the fight against the powerships was to use the government's layers of bureaucracy and over-regulation against it, slowing down the plan's implementation by insisting on detailed interdepartmental review. LIMS knew that this process would likely kill the plan outright.

Next, LIMS turned its focus to disseminating research that shared a very important fact about electricity production: private factories built on land can supply electricity at half the cost of the powerships, which were contracted out from Turkey. LIMS explained that the Lebanese government didn't have enough money to buy the fuel for the powerships and barges even if the equipment was offered for free, as the Ministry of Energy had already exceeded its budget for 2018.

Not only were these powerships inefficient and more costly than private, land-based production, but they also came with a heavy environmental cost. LIMS shared the stories of residents of the town Zouk Mikael, who have long complained to the government about the health problems from the existing powerships. Under the government's proposal, additional powerships would have been stationed in the same area, which would have doubled the suffering of the local population.

If private companies can supply better, cheaper service, it follows that government shouldn't control power production, instead opening up the market for others to compete. That's a better outcome for the people of Lebanon—and LIMS made sure the public heard this truth loud and clear.

Key Insights

LIMS proves that big policy fights are winnable, especially if the problem you're seeking to address has a significant impact on the general public. LIMS's story offers lessons on how to:

- Fill the void of new ideas with research and a fully developed set of solutions.
- Expose the public to your alternative vision and build public support.
- Leverage that public support and viable policy alternatives to create pressure on public officials.

Because LIMS was willing to speak out against further funding for the government's electricity monopoly, others were empowered to raise their voices, making the call for open markets louder and impossible to ignore. In addition to LIMS's policy research, the president of Lebanon developed a study quantifying the economic harm electricity outages and losses have caused and urged the government to pursue sweeping reforms.

LIMS followed up by stressing the importance of legalizing private generation and sales of power as opposed to further government spending on the sector, offering an alternative that would solve the country's electricity problem while costing taxpayers virtually nothing.

On Impact

LIMS won a decisive victory in the fight for electricity freedom, and their success is leading to better services and new reform opportunities. In October 2018, LIMS's advocacy helped oust an unaffordable new power barge the country had recently deployed. Momentum continued to build. The following spring, Lebanon's first privately-owned electricity company opened its doors, with much vocal support and celebration from the team at LIMS. On April 17, 2019, the Lebanese Parliament ratified a new electricity plan that slashes subsidies to the state-run electricity company and clears the way for private companies to produce electricity.

Discussion Questions

- How might LIMS's efforts to pass reform have been helped or accelerated by taking the time to identify and engage a broader coalition of groups supporting the reform?
- Oftentimes, what a think tank prevents from happening is just as important as the reforms it helps pass. What are effective ways or methods groups can employ to keep bad legislation or regulation from getting passed?
- How can think tank groups not lose sight of the big goal or reform while trying to achieve smaller wins that open up the potential for the "big" reform further down the line?

Clean Water for All

Asociación de Contribuyentes del Peru, Peru

Introduction

Peru is a country poised for a larger role on the global playing field. Formerly home to the oldest civilization in the Americas, dating back to the 32nd century B.C., Peru has most recently garnered attention as one of the fastest growing economies in Latin America. Diverse geography has provided an abundant range of natural resources, from mining to fishing to agricultural products, but the resources that fuel a broad scope of industries also lead to social strains.

Rapid economic growth of the past two decades has drawn about a third of the country's population of 30 million to Lima, the country's capital city. However, two-thirds of Peruvians are spread out across the country, from the coast to the mountains to the Amazonian rainforest.

This far-flung population makes it difficult to connect all citizens to the national economy due to an underdeveloped infrastructure in rural areas. While there are efforts to bring sanitation, medicine, telecommunications, and other elements of modern living to rural communities, the country is struggling to balance development and provide opportunity for all.

The structural and cultural barriers to development have resulted in opposing political narratives. In the 1990s, Peru began to pursue an approach of economic liberalization, ushering in investment and technocratic management of the country's economy. The same period saw stable inflation rates, steadily growing GDP, and an increasing number of trading partners. Some current political parties draw on this economic performance to advocate for increased liberalization. But others focus on the resultant inequality and press for schemes of redistribution, much in line with South American–styled socialism. The result of this philosophical clash will significantly influence the country's future.

Asociación de Contribuyentes del Peru (formerly Contribuyentes por Respeto) was founded in 2012 by a small group of lawyers, economists, and businessmen to defend the right of Peruvian taxpayers to receive quality state services in exchange for their taxes. This much-needed advocacy came at a time when, as Peru developed, the central government's coffers began to grow.

Due to a lack of understanding of appropriate development policy, billions of dollars were mismanaged and wasted. Asociación de Contribuyentes del Peru stepped in to help answer a simple question, "How can we unleash that investment to grow the country for all its citizens?"

Juan José García, one of Asociación de Contribuyentes del Peru's principal researchers who has been with the organization from the beginning, explained, "At the core of many problems in Peru are faulty institutions, which provides a ripe opportunity to conduct research and identify solutions." Garcia attributes his passion for employing free markets to solve problems to his experience working in the stock market when he was a teenager, along with his university studies, during which he discovered the Austrian School of economics. He is one of Asociación de Contribuyentes del Peru's four full-time employees.

Due to its small size, the organization must be lean and efficient, which has required an organizational strategy. This has been provided by José Ignacio Beteta, who joined as Asociación de Contribuyentes del Peru's president two years ago and has a background in leading other nonprofits. He expounded, "On one side, we have to be very prudent with resources; on the other, we have to take some risks to leverage for success in the future."

One way the organization has navigated that balance is partnering with another nonprofit to share back-office support to coordinate accounting, human resources, taxes, and paperwork. Garcia noted, "As a researcher, these changes have dramatically freed up

117

my time. I used to get stuck crafting Facebook messages. Now I can focus exclusively on my research."

In addition to its organizational acuity, Asociación de Contribuyentes del Peru benefits from exercising its identity as a one-of-a-kind organization. As the only taxpayers' association in Peru, being independent from both government and business sectors, the media has developed a deep interest in its work and perspective, leading to hundreds of mentions across radio, television, print, and online outlets. This widespread publicity has led to invitations by policymakers to weigh in on policy developments and positioned Asociación de Contribuyentes del Peru for effective advocacy.

Asociación de Contribuyentes del Peru's broad goal is to enhance free enterprise in Peru. All their research and analysis revolve around the interaction of the public and private sectors and how that impacts the daily lives of Peruvians. Being small and flexible, the team employs a range of tools to accomplish its mission, including original research, partnerships, and even cartoons.

Project Narrative

As Asociación de Contribuyentes del Peru strategized how to craft their "Leveraging Indices for Free Enterprise" (LIFE) project for Atlas Network, researchers cross-referenced current government initiatives, Peru's areas of weakness in global indices, their own scholarly aptitudes, and hot topics in society. What emerged as the nexus of these areas was one element: infrastructure. Specifically, they launched "Infraestructura para Todos" ("Infrastructure for All"), a campaign to pursue policy changes in telecommunications and water management, along with several smaller areas, that was designed to produce marked improvement in the World Economic Forum's *Global Competitiveness Report*.

Infrastructure is the skeleton upon which the economy is built, and typically, government plays the central role in its development. This is especially true in Peru because its relatively undefined institutions have prevented the provision of robust market-based public goods.

This gives rise to a dilemma because the most problematic factor for doing business in Peru, according to the World Economic Forum, is inefficient government bureaucracy. Additional problematic factors include corruption and the inadequate supply of infrastructure.

The population of Lima has increased by 50 percent over the past 20 years. Making matters worse for infrastructure development, rapid growth has meant that public investment dollars have been centralized around the urban core, further leaving the rural areas out of development initiatives.

Asociación de Contribuyentes del Peru's goal has been to transform this situation by freeing up latent capital and unleashing the solution-seeking power of the private sector as a way to drive development. "We started this project trying to release public-private partnerships (PPP)," said Beteta. PPPs are intended to blend the best of both worlds: drawing on public funding collected via taxes to provide public goods more efficiently through the market process.

The project goals included the following:

- Reduce civil society and local government's opposition to the installation of cell towers in key districts.
- Increase public awareness on the need to invest in water reservoirs through public-private partnerships (PPP) and not public-owned companies in order to secure water provision.
- Position the fact that there are companies executing PPPs on infrastructure projects under ethical standards in order to promote the use of PPPs in the reconstruction process.
- Design a program aimed at enhancing transparency in the reconstruction of highways where public resources are used.

In the past 10 years, access to mobile telephone networks in Peru has exploded, from around 30 percent to nearly 100 percent. This rapid expansion has caught some by surprise, particularly in rural communities where rumors of antenna-induced cancer have gripped people with fear, spurring opposition to further installations.

119

Coverage does not equate to quality, however, and while the vast majority of the country has some access to cellular networks, constraints on speed and reliability have limited the benefits associated with greater connectivity. Highlighting this point, one of Asociación de Contribuyentes del Peru's research reports explains that there are 289 antennas per million people in Lima, compared to 10,112 per million in Tokyo.

Asociación de Contribuyentes del Peru has adopted a tandem approach to advancing telecommunications reform.

First, they have published a number of studies that identify municipal practices and government regulations inhibiting the installation of cell towers. They analyzed 42 local governments, aggregated the findings on a website, and integrated them into social media campaigns.

Second, the Asociación de Contribuyentes del Peru team has partnered with the Ministry of Telecommunications to visit remote and mountainous areas of the country to explain the value of increased network expansion and to assuage fears of locals. "In Peru, many people are afraid of cell towers. They are worried about cancer and devaluation of property values," said Garcia. For this campaign, they developed the slogan, "Mas Antenas, Mejor Comunicación" ("More Antennas, Better Communication").

Their efforts have not been universally appreciated. In many inland areas, Peruvians speak local languages, imposing language barriers to Asociación de Contribuyentes del Peru's advocacy. Some cities have been open to the ideas presented, while others have gone as far as to kick the team out of the town. "This can be scary," recalled Garcia. Nonetheless, the project made gradual progress—until El Niño Costero struck.

Peru suffered extensive flooding and landslides (over 100 people died) in early 2017 due to an anomalous series of storms that impacted much of the economy and brought policy reform to a crawl. The aftermath derailed some of Asociación de Contribuyentes del Peru's efforts because public attention was diverted, but it also offered an unexpected opportunity: much of the nation's infrastructure stock was destroyed in the storms, resulting in "an ideal time to discuss (with policymakers) how to do the rebuilding," according to Beteta.

Over 9 million people in Peru do not have ready access to potable water. Water infrastructure is managed by public companies that are appointed by the rural government leaders. They are unbound by market pressure, and Peruvians suffer because of poor performance. However, due to the structure of nepotistic government management, "We have been unable to gain ground in advocating for private sector management of water," said Beteta.

Upon further research, Asociación de Contribuyentes del Peru discovered they could get their foot in the door of the water management industry by focusing on an individual stage of the process. They identified water sanitization as an undesirable but critical function of the water management process, often ignored by public companies and local politicians.

The El Niño Costero natural disaster vaulted this issue to greater prominence because the local water systems were overloaded and the inefficient management companies could not keep up. Seizing the opportunity, Asociación de Contribuyentes del Peru launched an advocacy campaign to allow PPPs in water sanitization. Relying on Asociación de Contribuyentes del Peru research, "we proved that many of these water enterprises were very much in debt," said Garcia.

The combination of urgency and research-backed advocacy prompted the central government to establish special procedures for water companies to proceed through bankruptcy and then restructure in a way that allows for the private sector to bid on management projects. This may take several years to become operational, but the process has begun. Asociación de Contribuyentes del Peru is optimistic. "The most important thing for us as a result of this achievement," noted Beteta, "is that we have become an established authority on policy reform."

A key factor that has slowed Asociación de Contribuyentes del Peru's progress in achieving reform in water infrastructure, and other areas, has been public reticence toward PPPs. Around the time the LIFE program began, a corruption scandal was emerging in Brazil that had repercussions across Latin America. The Lava Jato ("Operation Car Wash") scandal was a widespread corruption scheme whereby the publicly owned oil company Petrobas accepted bribes in exchange for awarding inflated contracts to private construction companies, tarnishing the reputation of PPPs around the world.

This challenge took Asociación de Contribuyentes del Peru by surprise. Beteta explains, "At the beginning, we were naïve. We didn't recognize the degree to which PPP could be used for corruption." Now, they have to expend efforts and resources to clean up the image of PPPs on top of their work to advance their implementation. This extra effort, however, has demonstrated that Asociación de Contribuyentes del Peru is willing to go the extra mile to demonstrate the merits of their policy recommendations.

Serving as an advocate and watchdog for PPPs, Asociación de Contribuyentes del Peru buffers against misbehavior on both sides. The government is compelled to allow PPPs based on the quality and reach of Asociación de Contribuyentes del Peru's research on the value of integrating free enterprise into the provision of public goods. Additionally, the business community is held in check because its practices are being monitored, resulting in less opportunity for corruption and greater chance of getting caught and punished. In this way, Asociación de Contribuyentes del Peru is positioned to spur on the private provision of infrastructure that is able to last beyond the bounds of the LIFE project.

One drawback of Asociación de Contribuyentes del Peru's rising status are the attempts from both government and business to appropriate their efforts. Policymakers have begun to rely on their research, involving them in the policy development process. "They have started asking for our help in writing reports and laws," Beteta revealed. While on the other hand, "private companies are starting to view us as partners . . . and they also want to have us as consultants." In each case, Asociación de Contribuyentes del Peru's most precious feature—its intellectual independence—is threatened.

The team navigates this challenge with tact, clearly conveying the importance of independence while reinforcing an interest to engage in cooperative pursuits. Such messaging has helped refine another of its capabilities, namely communication. This has, serendipitously, helped prepare them for challenges emerging from deep-seated cultural perspectives.

While Peru has maintained somewhat market-oriented policies over the past few decades, politicians have done a particularly poor job developing market institutions. This dichotomy has led to a sort of cognitive dissonance: Peruvians enjoy the benefits of a degree of market reform while they simultaneously have an affinity for socialism. In fact, people have an impression that markets are harsh, reflective of the past authoritarian regimes of Peru's own Fujimori and Chile's Pinochet.

As civil society, ungrounded in market principles, grows in power due to increasing wealth and access, Garcia and Beteta fear that the country may regress. They are especially worried about the Millennial generation, which esteems socialist values more than other groups and will form a cohort of 3 to 4 million eligible voters in the 2021 election.

Provoked to action by these statistics, Beteta reflects, "We need to translate our ideas in an emotional and romantic way." And that's just what Asociación de Contribuyentes del Peru is attempting to do. Presenting their research in simple language has been a core value since its inception. In fact, a defining element of their outreach is the use of cartoons to capture ideas and put them into a visibly accessible format.

The shift in demographics has prompted a further shift in media, so they are working to craft memes to specifically target Millennials. Garcia notes, "I am personally evaluating how to build a vlog to communicate ideas, hoping to develop tools to reach Millennials with ideas since they won't read a paper."

Asociación de Contribuyentes del Peru has proven to be an effective taxpayer advocate. Despite the series of major challenges Peru has faced in the past few years, the country has seen improvements in its rankings in the World Economic Forum's *Global Competitiveness Report*. The infrastructure score increased specifically in individual areas like mobile telephone subscribers and the quality of electricity supply.

Regarding telecommunications, the central government has become supportive of Asociación de Contribuyentes del Peru's policy recommendations, resulting in the Ministry of Telecommunications traveling with them to advance their policy education around the country. So far, they have visited nearly 30 percent of the regions. They also gained partnerships with civil advocacy organizations, multiplying their impact. Their boots on the ground campaign to expand the cellular network and in-depth analysis of bureaucratic barriers in the industry have contributed to Peru's improvement in the number of mobile phone subscribers.

Asociación de Contribuyentes del Peru's research and advocacy related to water management, and the associated triage of the country's views of PPPs, have contributed to Peru's ongoing discussion of this issue. Importantly, the government passed a law in 2016 that formally allows private companies to bid on water management projects.

Asociación de Contribuyentes del Peru began the LIFE project by focusing on "Infrastructure for All," looking to unleash the power of free enterprise in Peru to bring prosperity to the farthest corners of the country. They faced unexpected challenges along the way, being forced to change project aims midstream and build communication capabilities previously lacking. Throughout the process, the organization built its reputation. Maintaining a focus on the core pursuits of quality research and tactical communication efforts, it has become a trusted voice in public policy discussions.

Participating in the LIFE project not only helped Asociación de Contribuyentes del Peru focus its portfolio of initiatives and effect real change on the country's international rankings, it also helped the young think tank develop. "The LIFE program was the impetus to our success," explained Garcia. "Without it, we wouldn't have accomplished what we have."

Key Insights

On Building Relationships

The social and political environments in Peru pose challenges for anyone seeking to unleash the transformative power of markets. Nonetheless, Asociación de Contribuyentes del Peru has remained focused on understanding others' positions and finding ways to align opponents' incentives with their own. This has resulted in more invitations to be involved in crafting policy approaches, a longer-term win.

On Being Nimble

The impact Asociación de Contribuyentes del Peru has had is almost unbelievable considering they only have four full-time employees. The team has shown a remarkable affinity for building partnerships across a wide range of pursuits. Whether sharing back-office support with another nonprofit or starting a website in conjunction with a trade association, traveling to remote areas of the country with central government ministries, or engaging in disaster response discussions with international NGOs like the World Bank, Asociación de Contribuyentes del Peru has shown versatility in finding common ground and working toward the mutual benefit of many parties.

On Seizing Opportunities

Before Asociación de Contribuyentes del Peru, there was no taxpayer advocacy group in Peru, and there were many reasons to doubt that one could succeed. Yet armed with a vision for a more prosperous society, Asociación de Contribuyentes del Peru was launched, and it has met challenges such as natural disasters and political scandals related to proposed policy solutions head on. When politicians have been content with the status quo, Asociación de Contribuyentes del Peru has seen opportunities to push for policy changes, difficult as it might be. Its optimism is a great strength for an organization with limited resources in a challenging environment.

On Being Principled

Asociación de Contribuyentes del Peru set out to be a voice for taxpayers, and they have remained dedicated to that vision. The lure of increased impact if partnered with government or of greater financial stability if partnered with businesses have no doubt been present, but Asociación de Contribuyentes del Peru has stayed true to its original mission. This has in turn reinforced its reputation, leading to both greater influence and better financial standing.

On Staying Focused

Every success it has achieved has rested on the quality of its research. They have reorganized operations, partnered with wide-ranging groups, and pivoted to completely new issues, but they have always maintained principal focus on the quality of their research. Garcia confirmed the preeminence of this approach, saying, "We strive to be very solid in our research so we can withstand critique."

Discussion Questions

- What unique challenges has your organization faced? Asociación de Contribuyentes del Peru dealt with both internal and external shocks when executing its programs. How has your organization experienced something similar and how did you respond? Did the "fight or flight" instinct win out?
- What administrative or bureaucratic issues impede the development and reach of your work? How might your organization be able to find an outside-the-box solution to improve short-term performance while setting up for a stronger future?
- What is your comparative advantage? Is there one thing that your organization does better than anyone else, or that you would never stop doing? If it is an integral part of your organizational identity, how can you leverage this strength to have a greater impact?

- Would your organization be willing to partner with another organization that may disagree with you more than it agrees with you? In which areas could you see this being possible? What would it look like?
- Asociación de Contribuyentes del Peru has gained a lot of credibility by identifying (and acting) as an advocate for taxpayers. What messaging approach can your organization employ to win in the forum of public opinion? Have you ever tried to do this? What happened, or what do you think would happen?

SECTION VI
Case Studies on Unfair Tax Burdens

All tax regimes should observe fundamental principles of taxation. They should be broad-based, meaning the burden should be widely distributed, and neutral, meaning they should not favor one group or industry over another. Too often, government policy, often at the urging of special interests, seeks to use the tax system to manipulate markets or achieve narrow outcomes.

Those efforts threaten to create a litany of perverse unintended consequences. For example, a tariff on computers in Argentina was intended to protect a few domestic computer companies from competition, but the consequence was that everyone had to pay two to three times more for laptops, tablets, etc. than people in neighboring countries. This policy favored a few at the expense of everyone else. An even worse consequence is that higher prices disproportionately affect low-income populations.

Considerations for tax fairness have to include careful recognition of the unintended consequences of market-distorting policy. Too often, those consequences disproportionately affect low-income populations and prevent their full participation in economic opportunities.

Versions of the case studies in this section are available at AtlasNetwork.org.

Removing Barriers for Women

Advocata Institute, Sri Lanka

Introduction

Until recently, the Sri Lankan government taxed feminine hygiene products at over 100 percent, making a basic necessity unaffordable for most women in the country. In spite of a culture of silence and scorn surrounding this issue, the Advocata Institute bravely stepped up to become the voice for the voiceless when no one else would. Advocata's work not only started an important conversation but also led to a drastic reduction in the sanitary napkin tax, which stripped women of their dignity by preventing access to a basic necessity.

Advocata Institute's vision for Sri Lanka is that the country becomes more free, open, and prosperous. The organization's work aims to create a Sri Lanka with an abundance of opportunity for anyone to work hard and succeed.

In a country with 4.2 million women, only 30 percent use sanitary napkins. Instead, they resort to using cloth rags, which present sanitary and health concerns. This injustice went unchallenged for years because the female menstrual cycle is considered "unclean" and off limits by many in Sri Lanka. Women are often unwelcome in their homes and at school while menstruating.

The Advocata Institute took on Sri Lanka's culture of silence with a microphone, disseminating groundbreaking research on unjust taxation until government officials were forced to take action. Thanks to Advocata's efforts, the 30-percent import tariff on feminine products in Sri Lanka was eliminated. The total tax on feminine products has been reduced to about 63 percent from the previous 101.2 percent, and Sri Lanka's finance minister, Mangala Samaraweera, told the

Thomson Reuters Foundation he was looking into how taxes on sanitary products could be reduced further.

Here's how Advocata's work inspired change in Sri Lanka:

- The Advocata Institute succeeded in making sanitary napkins more affordable by ending the 30-percent import tariff on these products.
- Advocata's research exposed the barriers many women face in Sri Lanka, shining light on the issue and starting an important conversation on the need for change.

Advocata's story offers lessons on how to:

- Move the needle on economic reforms that may seem off limits because of cultural stigmas
- Be an authentic voice for change.

Advocata's success was a win for free markets and women alike in Sri Lanka.

A United Nations study found 60 percent of teachers in Sri Lanka think menstrual blood is impure. Because of this, 60 percent of girls are absent from school once a month during their cycle. Women are often forced from their homes during their period—some die, others face illness. All are subject to isolation and discrimination.

In short, women are stripped of their dignity because their culture does not like to deal with the natural female menstrual cycle.

This obtuse view on femininity is not only prevalent in the Sri Lankan society, but also permeates the way government levies taxes on feminine products.

"Women in South Asia generally face a culture of silence dictated by injustice and misogyny," said Anuki Premachandra, research communications manager at Advocata. "[As a nation], we are far from where we once were, but we have a long way to go. The role of a women is still widely seen and confined to the role of a caregiver, and the battle to defy this norm is one that we fight daily. Although the country was first to have a female prime minister, women are not seen as often as they should be in leadership and political roles. This is quite possibly also why high taxes on an essential like sanitary napkins exist and haven't been challenged by anyone until the Advocata Institute shed light on the numbers."

Project Narrative

Advocata knew that limited access to sanitary napkins was harmful, but they needed to know why and how it was affecting women.

Because of the sensitive nature of the fight, the group wasn't able to leverage human stories to explain why the issue is so important. They had access to data on girls missing school because of their periods and general attitudes toward menstruation from UNICEF and other groups—but they knew they needed more.

To that end, Advocata commissioned a consumer survey to learn more about how limited access to sanitary napkins was affecting women in Sri Lanka. What they learned was that at least 50 percent of low-income women did not use sanitary napkins.

Alternatives to sanitary napkins, such as cloth rags, are unsanitary and unsafe, but because of the cultural stigma surrounding women's reproductive health, policymakers are unaware of how this unhealthy alternative affects women. Poor hygiene caused by rags can lead to cervical cancer, which is the second-most-common type of cancer among Sri Lankan women. According to the HPV Information Center, current estimates indicate that every year, 1,721 Sri Lankan women are diagnosed with cervical cancer, and 690 die from the disease.

"The mere fact that a necessity as this is taxed so high goes to show how misrepresented women are in the real world here," Premachandra said. "We grow up in a culture where the topic of menstruation and womanhood is hidden and not embraced. A tax burden like this only does more injustice to a woman's dignity."

Armed with the facts and more detailed insight into the issues plaguing Sri Lankan women, Advocata was able to zero in on effective messaging and a persuasive argument on why the country needed to reform the way it taxes feminine products.

Sri Lankan cultural oppression of women goes beyond taxes on feminine products, and this affects the country's overall economy, in addition to impairing female upward mobility. For example, it is illegal for women to work later than 8 p.m. Restricting women's freedom and right to earn a living is incredibly harmful to half of the Sri Lankan population, and Advocata has stepped up as a voice for them.

They're able to put their money where their mouth is because most of Advocata's paid staff is female.

"I think having women on our staff has probably helped with sustaining the issue long term," said Deane Jayamanne, co-founder and director of Advocata.

Because of the diversity of the team's staff, they think differently. For example, Advocata came across the problem of high taxes on feminine products while researching taxes on diapers.

"I became a father almost two years ago and noticed that diapers in Sri Lanka were more expensive than the United States," Jayamanne said. "It's so expensive there's an underground mommy network of diaper smugglers. The researcher who was looking into tariff reform already did some digging and found out that there was a 62-percent tax on diapers, and while doing that we also discovered there was a 100-percent tax on sanitary napkins. We released the data to some media organizations and the issue shot up from there."

With female leadership like Premachandra championing women's economic issues, it became a natural fit for Advocata to take the lead in the fight for reform. Jayamanne says he has learned that when the issues his group champions have a "personal resonance," the chance of success is much higher.

"I do really think having diverse people in the room really makes a difference and opens up new areas and ways of thinking," he said.

Spreading the word on Sri Lanka's extreme taxation of feminine products created a monsoon of outrage on social media.

Attempting to harness and grow digital reach to spread the word on Advocata's campaign was new territory for the organization. The team did not have an exact science or understanding on how to leverage the new medium at first—one major challenge was identifying their target audience so their efforts on social media weren't aimed at a black hole.

Social media became important in this fight because other, more traditional, efforts based on research were not fruitful. But when Advocata took the issue to the people, perceptions changed. Once Advocata was able to tap into an audience that cared about the feminine products tax, they found they were able to fuel the fire for change by providing that audience with graphics, short posts, and videos that allowed the people to advocate for themselves.

Their tactics were successful. Public outcry caused the government official in charge of tax policy to examine the issue. Ultimately, he ended up cutting the tax.

"Freedom of trade will make goods and services related to female hygiene more available through this single reform," said Dhananath Fernando, COO of Advocata Institute. "Importantly, this will provide the opportunity for better the menstrual hygiene behaviors of females, who make up 52 percent of the population in Sri Lanka."

The tax reduction on sanitary napkins is an important step in a longer fight Advocata plans to tackle related to economic freedoms in their country.

Discussion Questions

- Are there minority populations in your country that are disproportionately harmed by bad government policy? What opportunities do you have to become a credible voice on their behalf?
- How would you prepare a compelling message around that issue?
- How can you ensure your team is benefitting from a variety of perspectives representing different walks of life in your country?

Beating Back Regressive Taxation
Lipa Taxpayers Association, Croatia

Introduction

Lipa is the leading voice for taxpayers in Croatia, advocating for their interests at all levels of government. The think tank's primary area of focus is on lowering Croatia's tax burden, which is 50 percent higher than the EU average, reducing the size of Croatia's government bureaucracy, and bringing more transparency to the system, as well as reducing public debt—a major driver of the country's high taxes.

Now in its third year, the young organization has already left a bold mark on Croatian civil discourse. The organization is totally reshaping the way citizens see the role of government in a land that has lacked a strong, independent, and people-focused voice for far too long.

Project Narrative

Lipa is a small shop, with just one full-time employee and a modest budget. Despite this, with grit and ingenuity, the organization stopped Croatia's new property tax dead in its tracks, unleashing such a powerful public backlash that Prime Minister Andrej Plenković was forced to repeal the tax in 2017 before it was ever implemented. Public outcry against the country's high tax burden has been so strong ever since that it has become virtually impossible to pass tax hikes of any kind in Croatia.

Lipa's campaign stirred the entire nation, awakening a latent desire for agency and freedom that had not been voiced publicly in many years. Lipa's volunteer campaign to spread the word on the anti–property tax movement yielded incredible results.

- Lipa's petition collected more than 20,000 signatures in the first 24 hours and reached 50,000 signatures in the first two weeks. When citizens started receiving forms from their local authorities asking them to give a detailed account of their properties, signatures then surged to more than 146,000 people, roughly 3.5 percent of the population.
- More than 100 news outlets covered the property tax repeal campaign, making it impossible for officials, residents, and influencers to ignore the grassroots momentum in favor of abolishing the new property tax.
- On September 14, 2017, the Croatian government fully repealed the nation's property tax. Despite multiple attempts since then, the current government has been unable to introduce any new taxes in the face of public opposition.

Lipa's phenomenal success has numerous lessons that can offer guidance to other free-marketers looking to do good work in their home countries. The organization's defeat of the Croatian property tax offers insight on how to:

- Build a grassroots movement
- Leverage public sentiment and the political climate to fight back against bad tax policy
- Speak in the language the target audience consumes.

Since becoming an independent nation in 1991, Croatia has seen market reforms take root, slowly but surely, but it hasn't been easy.

One way Croatia's men and women have exercised their new-found liberation since parting ways with communism is by investing in property. In fact, nearly 90 percent of all Croatians live in property they own—not rent—regardless of their income level.

Owning a home has become a powerful tool for investment and long-term stability as the maturing population deals with how to save for the future.

A property tax would have devastated this arrangement. But Lipa's brave team stood up against this toxic policy proposal to unite the country and, for one of the first times in independent Croatia's history, gave all citizens a voice.

Although Lipa was responsible for killing the implementation of a specific tax, their real success was in creating a movement of unity and hope, in which a people long held down by the strong arm of communism finally found their voice in the fight against taxes.

Croatia is in the midst of a demographic crisis. After seeing its population peak at 4.8 million in 1990, the country has experienced population losses every year as Croatians have fled the country for greener pastures in Germany, Ireland, and other European nations. In addition, the number of deaths has outpaced the number of births. Today, Croatia's population hovers at 4.2 million. In 2017, there were nearly 20,000 more deaths than births, and 57,000 Croats left for Germany alone.

Why? Crippling taxes and a weak economy. Croatia's personal income tax rate is 40 percent, and though this represents a decline from its peak of 56 percent in 2009, the income tax is still a significant problem, especially when combined with a 25-percent sales tax. With unemployment at 13 percent, and 40 percent for youths, the hope of planting roots and building a thriving future is not in the cards for too many Croats.

In 2016, a new tax reform package offered a glimpse of how things could change for the better. Toward the end of 2016, the Croatian government passed, and Parliament adopted, sweeping cuts to the country's personal and corporate income taxes. This was great news—but unfortunately, there was a catch. In addition to these cuts, the new legislation introduced a tax on property in Croatia that would have been devastating to the country. Nearly 90 percent of Croats own the home in which they live, meaning rich and poor alike would've felt the pain. Housing has been a key savings vehicle across the country dating back to communist rule, which offered one of very few avenues in which to save money under that system.

Lipa, which supported the tax cut portions of the legislation, knew it must act quickly and launched an innovative, anti–property tax communications onslaught. Because of the pressing nature of the issue—the property tax would have been effective January 1, 2018, had it been allowed to go into effect as planned—the organization leveraged multiple communications channels and approaches to reach Croats of all ages.

Before going public with their fight against the property tax, Lipa commissioned Velimir Sonje, one of Croatia's most influential economists, to provide an analysis showing how this new tax would affect the Croatian people. With those findings in the context of the overall tax burden, Lipa launched a marketing and communications campaign to help all Croatians understand what was at stake.

Armed with the facts, Lipa's campaign kicked off on April 18, 2017, with a press release that all major Croatian media picked up. In addition to the press release, the group shared an online petition against the introduction of the tax. Within 24 hours, more than 20,000 people signed the petition, and by the end of the campaign's first week, that number had jumped to 50,000 signatures.

The key to Lipa's rolling success and growing influence on the issue was its practice of using information to build the campaign and target more and more homeowners. No piece of collateral was a one-off—it was always repurposed, recycled, and recharged. For example, all media coverage of the campaign was promoted on Facebook, where Lipa has an active and influential audience of more than 15,000 followers.

Not everyone Lipa wanted to reach is a social media user, and not everyone tunes into the news stations Lipa was reaching. So they developed an anti–property tax petition to collect mailing addresses. As the number of signatories rose, so did the mailing list, which Lipa used to reach homeowners with newsletters and other mailings.

Momentum continued to build as separate milestones regarding the government's planned implementation of the property tax took place. The most significant peak in the campaign came in August 2017, coinciding with the point at which Croatian citizens started receiving forms from their local government authorities asking property owners to give a detailed account of their properties. This invasive move triggered an additional 100,000 people to join the campaign, applying even more pressure on the government. Many agitated property owners held protests in four major Croatian cities.

Finally, on August 8, the public outcry was unavoidable. Prime Minister Andrej Plenković pledged to withdraw the new property tax, signaling a win for the Croatian public and a major victory for Lipa.

Metrics of Success—Measuring Impact with Data

- A total of 146,100 signatures were gathered, which makes the petition one of the most successful civil-sector campaigns in the history of the Croatian democracy.
- According to Lipa's economic impact analysis, the organization's defeat of the property tax will mean Croatian citizens will keep 300 million kuna (US$50 million) more in their pockets instead of transferring that wealth to state coffers.
- Lipa's campaign totally shifted national sentiment on taxation. After the property tax failed, the Croatian government tried to introduce other new taxes but had to withdraw these proposals due to public resistance that came mainly from the people who signed Lipa's petition and continued receiving the group's newsletter. Lipa gathered 30,000 signatures against four new taxes one month after the property tax campaign. All of these new tax proposals were defeated.
- During Lipa's six-month fight against the property tax, 100 different national and local media published news on the campaign.
  - Lipa's members discussed the need of withdrawing the property tax law in 20 major TV appearances.

- Lipa's website experienced 380,000 visits in this period.
- Lipa's Facebook reach was 900 percent higher and added 50 percent more followers during the campaign.
- More than 350 people volunteered to collect signatures for the campaign.

Key Insights

On Crafting a Message

Fighting back against the government is never easy, but it's especially difficult when you're trying to stop bad tax policy without being able to clearly articulate to the public how much the tax would cost them.

When the Croatian government enacted its new property tax, a significant part of defining the new rate was left up to local authorities. On top of this, the way the tax would be calculated was a complicated formula based on property size and use, among other things.

In the end, the campaign won not because of numbers but because of Lipa's successful emotional appeal. The message that "A property tax makes us subtenants in our own homes" struck a chord with the people of Croatia and became a message that resonated with a vast swath of the population.

Why it matters: We have to work with the toolbox we're dealt. When data were not readily available for the anti–property tax campaign, Lipa was able to communicate the effects a property tax would have holistically, while also making an emotional appeal to a nation heavily invested in property.

Croatia's recent experience as part of communist Yugoslavia continues to have deep effects on its people and its economy, and this presented powerful opportunities as Lipa fought back against the new property tax.

One lasting impact that was particularly relevant for this fight was the effect of communism on homeownership in Croatia. Due to the inflation that was prominent under communist rule, people were forced to save money by purchasing properties, which did not lose value even as the value of national currency fell. Today, Croatia ranks

141

third in the European Union when it comes to rates of home owner-ship, after Romania and Slovakia. The country's high percentage of home ownership helped Lipa motivate citizens into action because the new tax policy directly affected their investments, which have come to have not only monetary value but also symbolic meaning and a strong emotional attachment.

On Inspiring the Public to Care

When Lipa first considered taking on the property tax fight, the team knew it would be an uphill battle. First, the EU Commission had recommended the measure as an appropriate decision for the government to pursue. Second, the general public had little to no knowledge about the property tax issue, let alone the intricacies and specifics of the federal legislation.

Before Lipa's campaign, Croatian citizens were generally not very sensitive to new taxes. They thought it was somebody else's problem—that taxation affects other, wealthier people.

So Lipa exposed the facts. The organization partnered with one of the nation's most respected economists to show how all Croatians would be affected by a property tax given the amount of revenue the country hoped the tax would generate, and it then produced com-pelling, consumable language to explain to the general public how every new tax directly means less money for them to spend on their families.

"The biggest lesson, and a positive one at that, was that it is pos-sible to get popular support on liberal topics in Croatia, if the cam-paign was done correctly—carefully choosing the messages and the communication channels for the target audience, timing it right and choosing the right topics," said Zoran Löw, executive manager of Lipa.

Why it matters: As policy wonks, we often feel that we have to "ripen an issue" to get anyone to care about what we're saying. And even in Lipa's case, when a major policy initiative was taking place in real time that would affect the vast majority of the country's residents, that challenge remained.

Why should anyone care? As much as personal messaging matters, you have to first start with the facts. Lipa did just that by putting a number on the economic impact of the property tax, then distilling this impact down to the simplest possible talking points and messages to expose the public to the danger of this policy.

Discussion Questions

- Lipa Taxpayers Association is a small organization, but regardless of its size, it was able to take on the government and stop the new property tax before it was implemented. How can other think tanks, advocacy groups, or nonprofit organizations with small staffs and/or modest budgets grow their advocacy efforts and expand the scope of their organization?

- The power of Lipa's campaign against the property tax had two parts: an economic analysis detailing how the tax would burden the Croatian people, and the marketing and communications campaign to help Croatians understand what was at stake. How can think tanks, advocacy groups, or nonprofits message their work in a way that resonates with people who may not understand the wonky details?

- Lipa's ability to engage their audience so quickly was due to their all-encompassing marketing campaign that targeted social media, radio, and direct mail—but that might not be the best strategy for all organizations. What things should other organizations consider when planning their marketing and communications strategy?

- An initial challenge that Lipa faced in its fight against the property tax was an unmotivated and unaware populace who did not understand how the new taxes would affect them. Aside from marketing campaigns, what can other think tanks, advocacy groups, or nonprofit groups do to engage new audiences who may otherwise stay unmotivated and unaware?

Section VII
Case Studies on Economic Freedom Audits

In cooperation with the Fraser Institute, publisher of the annual *Economic Freedom of the World* report, Atlas Network supports Economic Freedom Audits (EFAs), led by local think tanks, that convey the advantages of economic freedom to policy reformers. Each Economic Freedom Audit convenes a diverse set of stakeholders within the country to review and discuss local and regional country scores in search of consensus around priorities and opportunities for improvement. The three case studies in this section illustrate the process of identifying practical policy reform ideas, working with stakeholders, and developing strategies for implementation.

Versions of the case studies in this section are available at AtlasNetwork.org.

What Is an Economic Freedom Audit?

An Economic Freedom Audit is more than just a report or a ranking; it is an opportunity to gather experts to reach a broad, informed consensus toward institutional change. Local think tanks spearhead these audits and leverage their contacts and expertise to bring together media, businesses, government officials, and academic communities. After multiple meetings among important national stakeholders and the local think tank host, a final report is drafted and next steps identified.

A trained facilitator works with the various groups to engage feedback from participants in a way that stirs discussion while staying focused on the specific goals of the audit. Involving locals creates ownership and ensures the audit accurately captures reality because it is designed by people in the nation who understand their situation far better than outsiders do. The deep dive into each category provides real-time data on what is truly happening locally.

The report ranks the target country in the following categories: Size of Government, Legal System and Property Rights, Sound Money, Freedom to Trade Internationally, and Regulation. Each category has constituent parts, and each of those is scored. The report also lists policy recommendations, which are chosen after workshop discussions about each category. These discussions draw on cross-disciplinary perspectives to decide on key metrics of success, and this intensive process provides a richness that exceeds the natural constraints of the global EFW report.

The final report is not the sole product of the EFA process. Policy changes and sustained progress are the goals, and the results in the report are leveraged to garner media attention to impact public opinion and advance policy priorities in the target country. Media are engaged throughout the process, including preaudit news releases and interviews, transparent coverage of the audit process, a post-audit press release and more focused interviews, a final report that is full of detailed analysis and policy recommendations, and, ultimately, a formal presentation of the findings to the public.

Navigating a Crisis
Fundación Libertad y Progreso (LyP), Argentina

Buenos Aires, the capital of Argentina, is the most visited city in South America. Tourists enjoy its quaint streets, the old European feel, and the rich culture, but few of these visitors know that the country is in crisis.

The Argentine peso lost half its value in 2018, and Argentine equities and bonds lost significant value. The country has been in extended talks with the International Monetary Fund to secure a $57 billion deal that is the largest in IMF history. The country's central bank is striving to "re-establish confidence in the fiscal, financial, monetary, and exchange rate situation." But such reform may come at a price Argentines are unwilling to pay.

Workers regularly strike against attempts to curb salary increases, and people protest the austerity measures that have been presented. In recent years, however, people have become increasingly skeptical of the country's path, and they voiced their concerns by electing President Mauricio Macri in 2015, a business veteran and the first nonradical and non-Peronist president since 1932.

What will happen to the county has yet to be seen, but one organization is not content to sit on the sidelines waiting. Fundación Libertad y Progreso (LyP), a goal-oriented, free-market think tank located in Buenos Aires, has been actively engaging the disenchanted public with programs targeting policy reform.

Recently, LyP partnered with the Fraser Institute and Atlas Network to launch an Economic Freedom Audit (EFA), which provides a robust and in-depth evaluation of what exactly is pulling a country's economy down. The homegrown nature of LyP's audit produced concrete examples of various policies' direct impact on Argentines, capturing exactly what's wrong and honing-in on specific elements that can affect real change. The results of the EFA will serve as a roadmap for building a path out of the country's economic implosion. There have already been a few successes to emerge from the audit, and LyP's experience is instructive for other think tanks striving to motivate their own countries to escape stagnancy.

Country Background

To capture the gravity of the situation in Argentina, it is helpful to appraise just how far the country's fortunes have fallen.

The future for Argentina was once quite bright. In the early years of the 20th century, Argentina was one of the most promising nations on the globe, with one of the highest levels of prosperity and potential for rapid economic development, just like other rapidly developing countries like Australia, Canada, New Zealand, and the United States. In fact, many European immigrants debated whether to move to New York or Buenos Aires.

Now, those other countries vie for the top 20 spots in the Fraser Institute's *Economic Freedom of the World (EFW)* report, while Argentina has dropped almost to the bottom. The country has also fallen with respect to GDP per capita and is well below the world average, while its former peers all exceed 200 percent of the world average. In the report's latest edition, Argentina is one of the middle-to low-ranked countries.

This downward trend in Argentina began in 1943, when Colonel Juan Perón came to power after a military coup. Perón pursued the protectionist policies and economic nationalism of both Italian fascism and Latin American populism. *Peronism*, as the ideology of Perón and his successors became known, is characterized by corporatism, a focus on organized labor, and direct control and regulation of the economy. Perón was defeated in a coup in 1955, but the movement he started continued to develop, and populism persisted.

Argentinian populism created high demand for social services and fostered a skepticism toward the benefits of trade. In the 1960s, tariffs averaged 84 percent, and the state significantly taxed exports,

About LyP

Fundación Libertad y Progreso (LyP) is a nonprofit think tank based in Buenos Aires, Argentina. LyP fights for deep change in Argentina by working on the development of public policies, engaging in the national political discussion, and promoting participation by civil society in the debates surrounding the role of government in the economy. It strives to develop and advocate for public policies that will improve the quality of life in Argentina and the rest of Latin America in the long run.

LyP was formed through the merger of three like-minded think tanks that decided to unite to more effectively advance the common goals of respect of individual rights, limited government, private property, free enterprise, and peace.

LyP's activism has taken many forms. In 2017, its video about Argentina's high tariffs on laptops and tablets received 80,000 views and significant media coverage. As a result, the tariffs were repealed. LyP's tariff abolishment campaign came out of a report titled "An Open Argentina," which examined the state of Argentina's international trade and argued for trade liberalization. LyP also publishes its annual *Institutional Quality Index* (IQI), which lists and ranks countries according to the strength of their political institutions and level of corruption. (Argentina is ranked 119 out of 183 on the 2018 IQI.)

which shrank to 2 percent of national income. Government spending as a percentage of GDP more than doubled, from less than 10 percent in the 1930s to 30 percent in 2000 and 45 percent in 2015. Between 2003 and 2015, the number of public employees grew by 77 percent.

Populist policies sound appealing because they promise to provide generous benefits for daily needs. As an example, one policy guaranteed widows receive not only their own pensions but also those of their deceased spouse. If two widows who each receive two pensions move in together, they can claim "coexistence" with each other: if one of them dies, the other is eligible to claim all four pensions for the rest of her life!

These populist policies do not come cheap. In the decade between 2006 and 2015, Argentines paid $694 *billion* more in taxes than they did during the 1990s.

Many Argentines recognize the economic troubles that prevent prosperity, but they have learned that it is more difficult to put the genie back in the bottle; once a government bureaucracy begins to expand, it's difficult to restrain. In 2015, the newly elected government led by President Macri aimed to reduce the fiscal deficit and government expenditures, but that effort has been stunted.

With the terms of the new IMF bailout mandating stronger fiscal responsibility, including a prohibition on deficit spending and restrictions on currency manipulation, there's a chance Argentina will have enough motivation and accountability to stay the course. But simply meeting the loan requirements will have no permanent effect on the economy or daily Argentine life if not partnered with real, transformative, liberating policy change.

The Project

LyP wants to make the most out of the opportunity the current crisis presents. Because people may finally be interested in true reform, LyP wants to have solid policy recommendations prepared. To pursue this goal, they decided to conduct an Economic Freedom Audit (EFA) in conjunction with the Fraser Institute and Atlas Network. The purpose was to identify tangible obstacles to a healthy, thriving economy and develop solutions for moving forward— solutions that will be persuasive enough to convince their fellow citizens to support them.

"We believe increasing economic freedom in our country will lead to a new era of prosperity, reduced poverty, job creation, and growth," said Candelaria de Elizalde, the general coordinator of LyP. The objective is not just abstract policy change but improving the lives of everyday people. "Libertad y Progreso . . . has undertaken a project to analyze economic policies in Argentina with the objective of increasing economic freedom and thus the prosperity of Argentinians," explained Elizalde.

Together, the three organizations assembled a group of Argentinian stakeholders and top leaders to work on the project. Participants included a broad group of industry experts, including the former Minister of the Economy, the Vice President of the Central Bank, the Secretary of Political Economy, the General Manager of the Central Bank, the Secretary of Trade, and others. This level of involvement reveals a tacit acknowledgement that Argentina's leaders know there's a problem, that they are unsatisfied with the status quo, and are at least open to being involved in change. These are the building blocks of social change, and LyP wanted to make sure to capitalize on the opportunity.

In advance of the audit, LyP first contacted other organizations that had completed successful EFAs. Representatives at two other think tanks—the Samriddhi Foundation, a free-market think tank in Nepal, and Centro de Estudios para el Desarrollo (CED), a think tank based in Uruguay—shared in detail their experiences conducting an EFA. They also shared advice for conducting a successful EFA.

To establish a baseline for the audit, LyP dug into the nuts and bolts of Fraser's EFW materials, analyzing each component. For each audit, the Fraser Institute prepares a booklet that features the nation's level of economic freedom for each of the 42 variables in the index. To provide context for the results and to put them in perspective, the matrix also shows the scores of the top 10 nations for each variable, the top 10 average, the regional average, and the world average.

Fraser's dataset mostly comes from the *Doing Business* report from the World Bank, which measures the ease of doing business in 189 economies, and the *World Competitiveness Report* by the World Economic Forum, which analyzes 138 countries. By examining these materials, LyP ascertained Argentina's performance for each variable, how it compared to its neighbors and the world, and what improvements were needed.

After receiving advice and reviewing Fraser Institute materials, LyP commenced brainstorming for the multiday conference of the audit. They organized a series of seven workshops in a two-day event. The sessions focused on each of the components of the EFW index, with a few modifications. The Size of Government category, because of the particular challenges facing Argentina, was split into two sessions, the first considering public expenditures and the second taxation. The Regulation category was also given two sessions: Business and Labor, with the third element, Credit Regulations, being combined in the Sound Money session.

One important hurdle the LyP team needed to surmount was identifying where they should look for best practices to address the leveraged policy areas that needed improvement. They also needed to develop a cohort of attendees that would balance deep expertise and political knowhow. The success of the entire project, or any EFA for that matter, hinged on this. They had to get the right people in the room.

LyP held several meetings with internal project leaders and the organization's directors to determine which stakeholders to reach out to. By utilizing their extensive social and professional network, LyP sent invitations to targeted individuals and drew on the social capital that LyP's leadership had worked for years to establish.

Once the initial contacts had been made, follow up was delegated to a staff member. To help keep track of the status of invitations, the team used Salesforce, a customer relationship management (also called "CRM") software platform that integrates communications, analytics, and various automations that can significantly relieve administrative burdens.

This intentional approach attracted an impressive array of participants, ranging from the facilitator to the attendees for each topical session. Among the 46 workshop participants who attended, a cornucopia of professions was represented: academic economists, consultants, lawyers, public policy experts, elected officials, and economic policy analysts. Professor Martin Krause, a professor of economics at the University of Buenos Aires and an adjunct scholar at the Cato Institute, was the point person for the project and author of the final report. He also facilitated each of the workshop sessions.

To begin each session, Krause asked participants to introduce some key concepts of every issue. The topics raised covered wide and diverse policy areas, ranging from export duties on soybeans to off-budget government expenditures, rogue municipal governors to sanctioned investment vehicles for startups. The sessions provided key takeaways and opened discussion among the diverse participants, and the deep expertise of the attendees provided new ideas for policy reform for LyP to investigate further.

> **Challenge: Exogenous Shocks**
> Logistical issues can be unpredictable and yet disruptive. On the first day of the audit, a national strike brought public transportation to a halt. Similarly, on the day of the conference, Angela Merkel's visit to Argentina required increased security in Buenos Aires that restricted access to the meeting location. For these issues, LyP had to quickly develop and implement communication plans. Due to the organization's record keeping and use of CRM, contacting participants was significantly more efficient than it otherwise would have been. Such built-in tools and processes enable quick responses to unforeseen circumstances. Focusing on organizational nuts and bolts, while not glamorous, is sometimes what makes the difference between a project's success or failure.

Following the EFA, Professor Krause wrote a final report. Working with Fred McMahon, a resident fellow at the Fraser Institute who provided expertise on the EFA process, the two scholars built a communications plan to strategically distribute the results of the audit. Outreach included press interviews, meetings with policymakers and other leaders, and presentations in two cities, Buenos Aires and Tucumán. Notably, Krause and McMahon also met with representatives of the National Congress at the Friedrich Naumann Foundation's office. The representatives were impressed with the audit, its findings, and some of the policy recommendations, building opportunities for future engagement.

McMahon also gave presentations to Argentinian think tanks. He visited the Fundación Instituto David Hume to present to an audience of academics and professors who were unfamiliar with the Economic Freedom Index. And in Tucumán, McMahon spoke to a group of youth assembled by the Foundation for Federalism and Liberty (*Federalismo y Libertad*), a young think tank that for several years has been ranked as a "Top 100 Think Tank to Watch" by the University of Pennsylvania's *Global Go To Think Tank Index*. These in-person visits put actionable information directly into the hands of influencers involved in Argentina's policy formation.

From Plan to Policy: Workplace Reform

The importance of the audit lies not just in the report but also in serious policy outcomes and sustained ideological change. LyP can claim at least one policy win—so far—that has emerged from its audit. During the workshop on regulation, experts specifically debated Argentina's labor market regulatory scheme. According to the audit report, "When the cost of hiring or employing workers is too high, businesses are reluctant to hire. Creating jobs for future generations is a key priority for Argentina, and yet its own laws, regulations, and regulators stand in the way."

At the time of the report, Argentina's labor market regulations imposed high costs. In the "hiring regulations and minimum wage" audit category, Argentina scored 2.23 out of 10, and in the "hiring and firing regulations" category, scored a 1.9 out of 10. Overall, for the entire category of "labor market regulations," Argentina received 2.52 out of 10. For comparison, the United States scored 9.2, and the South American average was 5.3.

Discussion at the workshop revealed that the Macri administration had once attempted to ameliorate labor market issues through a "first job bill," which would have made it easier for 18- to 24-year-olds to find jobs. However, the House's Labor Committee never considered the bill.

The workshop exchange generated a series of considerations any labor reform would require.

- Argentina would need to return to "a culture of work." A good channel for returning to such a culture would involve transforming existing welfare programs into workfare by promoting work for those receiving social subsidies.
- The public sector must move its own excess employees into the private sector.
- The Law of Labor Contracts needs an update to account for increased flexibility resulting from technology.
- The right to strike needs further regulation to prevent excess.

Following the audit, LyP created a video entitled *Why Argentina Fails*, drawing on ideas developed in the workshops. The video highlighted employment and labor reform problems, explaining that 8 million Argentinians work to support 20 million receiving government payments. LyP won Atlas Network's Lights, Camera, Liberty Film Festival Award for its work and message.

Why Argentina Fails gained significant media traction, earning 420,000 views and catching the attention of Argentina's government. The government included some of the proposed reforms in its *Programa Empalme* (Connection Program), launched in June 2017, which subsidizes business with an average of $4,430 for each person they hire who was on social welfare. *Programa Empalme* is aimed at providing a path to productive employment. The subsidy lasts for two years of work, and businesses are restricted in the share of employees that can participate in the program. The program is currently in a beta phase, with 12,280 participants in the program. There is strong demand for a full rollout to extend to the estimated 70,000 potential candidates.

Programa Empalme is a promising policy that builds on the work presented in LyP's audit. Furthermore, it demonstrates that an audit is more than product; it is also a process to identify solutions and start a conversation. The program also shows that successful follow up can have tremendous results.

Key Insights

A unique challenge for LyP was figuring out how to motivate Argentines out of complacency. Early economic success established a comfortable way of life, and allowed the formation of numerous and visible public perks. But the unseen is what threatens to cripple the country. The country could continue many of its social welfare programs with slight reforms to please its international lenders, but this path would come at a great opportunity cost of what they could become.

LyP drew on individuals' aspirations for prosperity to build momentum for their EFA and the resultant policy recommendations. Appealing to this very personal concept by focusing on labor policy, something that affects nearly everyone in society and is crucial for policymakers, made the policy conversation practical rather than ideological. LyP found a pressure point that was close to home and used it as a catalyst to move toward broader change.

A successful audit can lead to serious policy changes and ideological shifts. Leveraging an organization's background and skills can set the stage for success, but it's only one part of the equation. Engaging a diverse and well-equipped body of participants is how to generate content and mobilize solutions. Combining these elements, along with the structural support of good business operations and a strong network of partners, increases the chances of a successful policy reform project. LyP's audit led to real policy solutions that could become the groundwork for more sustained, substantial change in Argentina.

Through the workshop and meeting process, experts and leaders drafted a series of necessary requirements that serious labor reform efforts ought to include. By coupling this research with a video campaign, it appears that the government of Argentina is acknowledging government bloat and taking actions to decrease it. The current *Programa Empalme*, while still in its early stages, shows that successfully implementing and following up on an EFA can achieve sustained ideological shift and policy change.

Discussion Questions

- How did culture impact the Overton Window that LyP faced? What are the cultural barriers that your organization faces when pursuing policy reform?
- What unforeseen events have hampered the success of projects you have worked on? Did you build in contingencies for future initiatives? If you did, what were they? If you didn't, could your projects be at risk from other unexpected variables?
- What is a way that LyP overcame blind spots?
- What technological or business process could yield immediate benefits to your work? What about in the longer term?
- What policy issue in your target market personally resonates with people and their everyday lives?

Redefining Freedom

Centro de Divulgación del Conocimiento Económico
para la Libertad (CEDICE), Venezuela

Venezuela was once the most prosperous country in Latin America. Much of this was due to economic freedom. In fact, in 1970 Venezuela had the highest level of economic freedom in Latin America and was 10th in the world, as ranked by the Fraser Institute's *Economic Freedom of the World* (*EFW*) report. Unfortunately, prosperity led to ill-advised social and economic policies. The combination of shifting commodity prices, rapidly expanding public employment, and restrictive economic policies resulted in stagnation and then decline, exacerbated by populist political leaders who continued to expand unsustainable social programs.

Poverty levels in Venezuela now exceed 90 percent. Grocery queues stretch around city blocks and require hours of waiting to purchase meager supplies with mountains of devalued currency. Venezuela is the now lowest-ranked country in the latest edition of the Fraser Institute's *EFW* report, coming in 159th with a score of 2.92 out of 10. Notably, those scores are from 2016, and conditions have gotten worse since then.

As millions flee to neighboring countries for hopes of a better life, one local think tank is digging in its heels and pressing for reform, striving to realize the hopes of millions of Venezuelans in their own country. CEDICE (Centro de Divulgación del Conocimiento Económico para la Libertad) is a nonprofit think tank that has studied the Venezuelan economy since 1984, when it was founded by entrepreneurs unsatisfied with the policy climate of the country. According to the 2017 *Global Go To Think Tank Index Report* released by the University of Pennsylvania, CEDICE is one of the top 100

About CEDICE

CEDICE views free-market principles and individual freedom as the basis for building a society of free, ethical, and responsible individuals. The organization strives for a free and prosperous Venezuela, where the lives and property of its citizens are protected. Through a diverse portfolio of activities—including economics programs for children, youth, and journalists; a Country of Owners program to promote the importance of private property; a Center for Ethics and Corporate Citizenship; and more—CEDICE fights for social and policy change. And the organization is remarkably effective.

In 2012, CEDICE won the prestigious Templeton Freedom Award for its journalist training program, which familiarizes media workers with classical liberal ideas and the broader CEDICE community. Venezuela has a long history of media repression, and CEDICE's work combats government crackdowns on journalism.

---

think tanks in the world, ranked ninth in Latin America, and has the 15th most significant impact on public policy.

CEDICE disseminates, teaches, and defends the principles of free markets and individual freedom, seeing these values as central to a flourishing society. The organization employs a diversity of programs to affect change, including an Economic Freedom Audit (EFA) designed to study in depth the core issues plaguing the Venezuelan economy and to develop policy solutions to get the country back on the path of freedom and prosperity for all.

Country Background

In 2018, economic freedom is almost entirely absent in Venezuela, with corruption, crime, and shortages of even the most basic goods afflicting the country. The country has seen a long and recently dramatic decline in economic performance and quality of life. But this was not always the case.

Rich in natural resources, Venezuela developed extensive agricultural ventures at the turn of the 20th century, exporting cocoa and then coffee across the globe, facilitated by free trade agreements. The economy later shifted to oil, which further attracted immigrant workers, who in turn fueled more economic growth. In the late 20th century, the city streets bustled with business and shopping, workers enjoyed higher wages than in any other country in the region, and newspapers contained advertisements for Chevy Camaros, which were manufactured in the country. International growth fed an oil boom that the country capitalized on due to possessing the largest oil reserves in the world. But the country's growth was not exclusively tethered to oil, and although oil prices declined in the 1960s, Venezuela's economy continued to grow.

Following this period of expansion, however, Venezuela began adopting heavy-handed government policies, including the establishment of economic planning agencies, agricultural land redistribution, price and exchange rate controls, tripling income taxes, and nationalizing numerous industries, such as the Central Bank and the oil industry. Yet even in 1980, Venezuela was still one of the richest and most economically liberal nations in South America, rated 13th by the *EFW* report—just behind Australia.

By 1990, the effects of bad policy were becoming more evident, with Venezuela falling to 53rd in the *EFW* ranking during the presidency of Carlos Andrés Pérez, who was later forced out of office and convicted of embezzlement of public funds.

Venezuela is a relatively young democracy, having only adopted universal suffrage in 1959, almost 140 years after independence from Spain. In that time, the country has had a variety of political and economic systems, with populist ideas often winning out. This has led to expansive welfare policies, which have ballooned over the years. Socialists and crony capitalists vying for control of a sinking ship have often realized short-term gains by taking on more water. Policies that sprang out of a booming economy and political aspirations are now a key factor hampering the economy.

In 2000, under Hugo Chávez, Venezuela's economic freedom continued its nosedive, reaching 88th place in the *EFW* ranking. Since 2005, Venezuela has been one of the least economically free countries in the world. Under its current president, Nicolás Maduro, Venezuela has increased the money supply without cutting government programs, leading the country into hyperinflation. The IMF expects the inflation rate to surpass 1,000,000 percent in 2018.

The economic crisis and inability of the government to meet its pledges has triggered widespread distrust of the government. Government leaders have further escalated the tensions. For example, Maduro's government banned two popular politicians, Henrique Capriles and Leopoldo López, from running against the incumbent president. In the last election, only 46 percent of Venezuelans even bothered to vote, a far cry from the over-90-percent turnout throughout the 1960s and 1970s. Political distrust has also taken other forms, and Venezuelans have fled into neighboring countries. Colombia has received more than half a million Venezuelan refugees in the last two years alone.

Due to economic and political instability, crime rates have skyrocketed. As of 2017, the capital city of Caracas is the second-most-violent city in the world, with 111 homicides per 100,000 residents. (As a comparison, the most violent city in the United States is Baltimore, Maryland, with a homicide rate of 56 per 100,000 people—approximately half as many.) The spike in crime has swamped the courts, with over 70,000 people currently awaiting trial.

While the majority of Venezuelans suffer, many wealthy, connected elites enjoy the privileges of cronyism, using the political system to enrich themselves at the expense of the entire society.

- From 1984 to 1994, President Jaime Lusinchi stole an estimated $36 billion in public funds.
- During his presidency, Chávez purchased a $65-million airbus, despite the purchase violating the constitution and other regulations.
- Currently, the Chávez family owns 17 country estates comprising more than 100,000 acres, and Chávez's daughter is the richest woman in Venezuela.

The Project

In light of Venezuela's rapid decline, it is difficult to capture a clear picture of what exactly is going on and how to get back on track. To address this issue, CEDICE conducted an Economic Freedom Audit (EFA) with the Fraser Institute and Atlas Network in 2016. The purpose of the audit was to identify specific obstacles to a healthy, thriving economy. EFAs are a brainchild of the Fraser Institute and Atlas Network, who have formed a partnership to assist think tanks in the poorest-performing countries in the *EFW* report. The Fraser Institute provides the evaluation expertise, while Atlas Network draws on its extensive global network of think tanks to make connections in the target countries.

Together, CEDICE, Atlas Network, and the Fraser Institute launched the EFA process for Venezuela. Carlos Goedder, a CEDICE economist and the coordinator of the Venezuelan EFA, explained that, "Our motivation was to verify the dimensions measured in the index, analyzing all the variables considered for the ranking, tracking their deterioration, and making sense of such significant underperformance."

Prior to beginning their audit, CEDICE staff connected with other organizations that had already successfully completed EFAs in other countries. Arpita Nepal, co-founder and research and

162

development advisor at Samriddhi Foundation, a free-market think tank in Nepal, shared her experience and advice for conducting a successful EFA. Gaining insights and learning best practices was an important step before launching such an intensive project. Early course correction and refinement, even before a project launch, is a key way to efficiently manage both resources and social capital.

Next, CEDICE downloaded the 42 individual variables that make up the country's *EFW* report score from the Fraser Institute (data are publicly available for 162 countries). Then it verified the results and examined the comparative ranking and historical performance of each variable. Fraser's dataset mostly comes from two reports, the *Doing Business* report by the World Bank, which measures the ease of doing business in 189 economies, and the *World Competitiveness Report* by the World Economic Forum, which analyzes 138 countries. Conducting the literature review and implementing its outreach plan to connect with local stakeholders and invite them to participate in the workshops took a total of five months, from March to July 2016.

Once the appropriate data was gathered, dates were set, invitations were sent, and the panels of experts began their reviews of each area of the index. From April to June, CEDICE contacted potential stakeholders and organized seven workshops, one for each category of the *EFW* report.

Challenge: Hurdles to Participation

Successfully gathering qualified participants was one of the key challenges CEDICE faced. Venezuela's economic and political situation is dire, and CEDICE encountered roadblocks when trying to gather stakeholders. Aside from normal logistical issues, residents of Caracas have many reasons to avoid attending. First, buying food or services is a time-consuming task, given shortages and long queues. Working hours are constrained, and going to a workshop with no financial compensation requires strong commitment. Second, some fear being identified as enemies of the government and its policies. In Venezuela, being considered a "contrarian" can result in losing a job, complications in receiving public services, and even potential sanctions and prosecution. Lastly, as already mentioned, Caracas has one of the highest murder rates in the world, and staying out past business hours is dangerous.

Recruited experts were grouped according to the different areas of the EFA. CEDICE guaranteed each expert confidentiality of opinions to avoid oppression by the Venezuelan government. Such security was a powerful incentive for turnout and attendance. During these workshops, representatives from 48 organizations discussed the interrelated aspects of economic freedom. Organizations included nonprofits, consulting firms, law firms, universities, unions, and even the Caracas Chamber of Commerce.

CEDICE's success in gathering stakeholders was due to the social capital it has built over the course of the organization's history. Since 1984, CEDICE has hosted numerous events and published well-known publications. They have also maintained a database of friends, endorsers, and interlocutors who consider CEDICE's work reliable and serious, even if they fundamentally disagree with the organization's political positions. The addition of other globally recognized organizations helped give the EFA further legitimacy to attract participants.

Ultimately, CEDICE gathered 108 different stakeholders to meet from July 25–28, 2016. Stakeholders included representatives, leaders, and entrepreneurs from universities, public agencies, unions, media, civil society organizations, banks, and companies. The attending individuals included experts with broad historical and quantitative knowledge, as well as individuals deeply embedded in their line of work, with important qualitative and tacit knowledge of their respective enterprise.

Challenge: Moving Faster than the Data
Another key challenge CEDICE faced was that the 2016 *EFW* report, which it was initially using, was based on data from 2014. This data would be accurate enough for most countries, but due to Venezuela's rapid and considerable

deterioration since 2014, there was a risk that reality was too divorced from the data in the report to be as useful in capturing the true economic state and generating applicable policy recommendations. As a result, CEDICE decided to postpone its report until the updated EFW data sources were published with data for 2016–2017. The new data were released in October 2016. Waiting for the updates caused a delay in CEDICE's planned rollout of the *EFA* report. However, CEDICE determined that the benefit of more accurate data outweighed this cost and provided better macroeconomic indicators. In the end, the updated data painted a grimmer picture of Venezuela, but it also provided a more reliable baseline upon which to build reforms.

To roll out the EFA workshops, the Fraser Institute's Fred McMahon joined the CEDICE team to implement the audit. He opened each session with a review of the performance of free economies and explained how they differ from Venezuela's economic system. McMahon was an important ally during the EFA, since he had already visited other countries for previous audits. Those at CEDICE were worried about the kind of reception someone from a high-profile think tank like the Fraser Institute would receive—after all, government officials and union leaders were attending the workshops—but McMahon's delivery of information from mainstream sources and good interpersonal skills endeared him to the audiences.

CEDICE and McMahon also visited the Economics and Sustainable Development Unit of the British Embassy in Caracas, which was interested in the report and further dissemination of the findings throughout the business community. Additionally, during the conference, McMahon visited Consecomercio, a nonprofit local trade association. There, he discussed the benefits of economic freedom with nearly 50 business owners and managers. Partnering with organizations that have deep experience and strong knowledge is a valuable way to support the rollout of a new project.

An important feature of the EFA is that the workshop discussions were not overly "wonky," or focused solely on examining purely quantitative data. To help supplement the numbers, individual citizens struggling through the repressive Venezuelan economy presented their own personal testimonies.

One participant, Oswaldo Bonillo, shared his story. Bonillo was the owner of a mechanical workshop that had been expropriated by the Venezuelan government in 2011. Although he was never formally sentenced or charged, the government seized his property with impunity. After 50 years of hard work, an arbitrary decision by a government agency robbed a man of his livelihood in a mere 48 hours. "I began to take notice of private property when I was the victim of an expropriation," said Bonillo during the workshop on the legal system and property rights.

Bonillo's story is not uncommon. According to the Observatory of Property Rights, sponsored by CEDICE, the Venezuelan government closed 28,000 private enterprises in 2015 and seized over 4 million square meters of private land. Bonillo was never compensated, and he has yet to hear from the judiciary.

"Owning private property is a crime in Venezuela," said one attorney attending the workshop. In 2015, there was an average of 256 attacks on small businesses per day. In addition, this disregard for private property is enshrined in Articles 115 and 116 in the Venezuelan Constitution, including the statute, "Property shall be subject to such contributions, restrictions and obligations as may be established by law in the service of the public or general interest."

A series of policy proposals to help increase Venezuela's property rights protection score and provide positive change to real people impacted by government takings emerged from these workshops. A group of law students suggested the creation of property courts. Currently, Venezuela lacks specialized courts to settle property disputes. Like Bonillo, those whose property is expropriated have no viable channel for legal recourse. These newly established property courts would return confiscated property and have the sole authority to grant expropriation orders. Furthermore, to help address the broader, cultural disregard for property rights, participants suggested the creation of housing titles for beneficiaries of housing subsidies, based on the idea that creating more homeowners could help imbue Venezuelans with respect for private property.

Speeches and discussions during the other workshops resulted in additional public policy proposals. The focus for these was on "quick wins," the kind of pragmatic adjustments that could have a big impact while being implemented with relatively few difficulties or costs. These small adjustments could result in marked improvements for the living standards of Venezuelans.

> **Challenge: Entrenched Views of Government's Role**
> A particularly challenging element of Venezuelan society is the propensity to favor government involvement in the economy. The EFA workshops revealed that this sentiment is firmly entrenched, even among those open to the idea of freer markets. CEDICE found that neither government bureaucrats nor the opposition parties believe in true liberalization, but rather they may only be willing to support softer government regulations and controls. CEDICE's previous work, like its journalist training program, has focused on changing the narrative toward the importance of business, liberalization, and entrepreneurs. Throughout the EFA, this was one reason for the focus on "quick wins."

To help engage with a potentially hostile audience at the workshops, CEDICE and McMahon wrote quick introductions that utilized facts, figures, and recent news to provoke and start discussion. For example, during the session on Sound Money, they collected and presented the most recent numbers on inflation, monetary base growth, and alternative measures of CPI inflation. This culminated in a proposal for the "dollarization" of the economy—a total pledge to the USD—similar to policies enacted by other South American countries. In a country with rampant inflation and a monthly minimum wage hovering around US$3, such an idea is attractive to a broad spectrum of audiences. In fact, once the Sound Money workshop concluded, union leaders requested photographs with McMahon.

A key to the success of the EFA was the willingness to hear all voices and not insist on ideological purity to draft policy recommendations. Although the ultimate goal is the dismantlement of exchange rate and price controls, short-term policies are also important, and providing an atmosphere of engagement has the potential to more effectively impact policy in the long term.

Additional policy recommendations included easing registration for private companies, unifying export/import documentation and tariffs in a single official webpage, privatizing nonstrategic assets under control of the government, and allowing a fraction of shares of public companies to list in the stock market, domestically or abroad.

Bonillo's story, the workshop discussions, and the participation in forming policy recommendations demonstrate the way CEDICE's EFA succeeded. The audit worked through the combination of expert testimony, quantitative data, personal stories, and policy proposals for each one of the categories defined in the Fraser Institute's *Economic Freedom of the World* report.

Key Insights

A successful audit can lead to serious policy changes and ideological shifts, so determining the factors that ensure success is crucial. From CEDICE's EFA, four important lessons arise.

1. CEDICE's researchers thoroughly understood the available data, even delaying rollout to ensure that their audit featured an accurate representation of their country.
2. CEDICE utilized the experience of its network to reach Venezuelan leaders across industries and spheres of influence. Allies, like the Samriddhi Foundation and Fred McMahon, had detailed experience regarding the requirements needed to make an EFA successful. Contacting others who have completed an audit is an easy way to learn from experience and avoid mistakes.

3. The stakeholders and leaders who attended the audits were qualified, experienced, diverse, and committed to change. CEDICE gathered stakeholders who were committed to liberalization and others who were initially hostile. The common thread was that everyone had gathered to rebuild their crumbling nation and offer ideas for how to improve both their own lots and the lives of their compatriots.
4. The presentations and speeches featured a balance of quantitative and qualitative material. People from different fields and industries filled the workshops, from professors to bureaucrats to union representatives—it was thus imperative to keep the sessions accessible to everyone to facilitate productive interaction.

The social and economic state of Venezuela has gotten worse than anyone could have predicted 50 years ago, and getting on the road to recovery is more important than ever. While present and future prospects are still dim, the fact that an Economic Freedom Audit was not only possible but had such strong participation is telling. Participation by leaders in Venezuela, ranging across sectors, demonstrates that citizens recognize the problems of a socialist regime and are willing to fight for change. The success of the EFA is also a testament to impact a small think tank full of hardworking and committed advocates can have when equipped with effective programs, operational expertise, and an actionable network of contacts.

The policy recommendations developed by the cross-partisan, diversely affiliated EFA workshops are a strong and positive first step toward returning Venezuela to prosperity. The report generated by the audit provides further intellectual credibility to CEDICE as it continues to push for social change. CEDICE's exemplary implementation of the EFA, in the face of great hostility, offers inspiration and a replicable playbook to other advocates of economic freedom.

Discussion Questions

- What project could your organization run that would not benefit your organization but could lead to measurable policy change? If your organization never gets credit for its work, is it worth it?
- How useful is data in developing policy change? Can you ever have too much data?
- What are some organizational partnerships that could help your organization better achieve its mission through collaboration? What does that collaboration look like in detail (e.g., who does which roles)?
- Can a country's economy reach a point of no return? If yes, how do you know when you're approaching that point? If no, why not?
- What sacrifices could your organization make that could encourage engagement by your target audience? Being less (or more) ideologically constrained? Do the ends justify the means?

Reasons for Hope

Egyptian Center for Public Policy Studies (ECPPS), Egypt

Water has brought prosperity to Egypt for millennia. The richness provided by the Nile River and fertile soil historically produced agricultural boons, but in modern times, an adjacent body of water has brought its own flood of commerce: the Suez Canal. Opened in 1869, the canal is an artificial waterway that connects the Mediterranean Sea with the northern Indian Ocean via the Red Sea. Each year, this allows 17,550 vessels (25-percent more traffic than the Panama Canal) to bypass up to 4,000 miles of sea travel in each direction.

Since opening, the Suez Canal has been a nexus for political power along with its promise of prosperity. Egypt is no stranger to political tensions. Since its history began, there have been powers vying for control—the Persians, the Romans, the Arabs, the Turks, and the British, to name a few. Outside parties have impacted the daily governance of the Egyptian people, for better or worse.

In recent years, it has become more possible to track the impact of political forces on the country's performance. Social scientists and international organizations seeking to unlock development have developed novel measurement tools to inform policymaking. One such indicator is the *Economic Freedom of the World* (*EFW*) report, generated by the Fraser Institute. Economic freedom is strongly correlated with other metrics of well-being for individuals and entire societies. The *EFW* index captures performance on a range of public policy indicators, which include Size of Government, Legal System and Security of Property Rights, Sound Money, Freedom to Trade Internationally, and Regulation.

Egypt has underperformed in each of these areas. In fact, Egypt is one of the lowest-ranked countries in the latest edition of the *EFW* report, coming in at 140 out of 159, with a score of 5.73 out of 10. In terms of personal freedom, Egypt is ranked 156th. This hasn't always been the case. While never ranking at the top of the report, Egypt was consistently near the middle of the pack until the past decade or so. In 2000, Egypt was ranked 72nd out of 123 for economic freedom, meaning that the country has fallen from the top 39 percent to the bottom 12 percent.

The inflection point can be tied to the Arab Spring. On January 25, 2011, Egyptians took to the streets of Cairo's Tahrir Square to protest for increased political and economic freedom. More than 800 died in clashes with police. The demonstration resulted in the removal of Egypt's longtime dictator, Hosni Mubarak. Out of the upheaval, Mohamed Morsi of the Muslim Brotherhood, arose as the nation's leader, but that was short-lived and led to further national turmoil, protests, and another regime change.

The government has long sought to appease the public with increased spending. Such policies have brought new kinds of plagues on the country: subsidies, inflation, and debt. Public debt has surpassed 100 percent of GDP. Fuel, water, and food are heavily subsidized. For example, Egyptians pay only 59 percent of the cost of fuel, and the state pays the rest (amounting to $30 billion over five years). These subsidies account for nearly one-third of Egypt's public expenditures—13 percent of GDP. This has led to market distortions in the economy, which has chilled investment.

Despite increased public spending, necessary institutions have broken down, and society has grown segmented based on people's connections to power. Under the table payments have become prominent, and poorly enforced laws and ingrained corruption leave some businesses dependent on leveraged connections and middlemen, while others are well connected and enjoy special treatment. In 2016, half of Egyptians who used public services paid a bribe. A quarter of businesses identify the current Egyptian court system as a major hindrance to their ability to do business in the country.

The international community has taken notice, and some groups have pursued constructive change. In 2016, the International Monetary Fund (IMF) initiated a $12 billion loan in accordance with the tranches that the Egyptian government requested. This has spurred some economic reforms. So far, the Egyptian government has:

- Floated its currency, untethering the Egyptian pound and allowing market forces to determine its value.
- Strengthened minority investor protections by increasing the rights of shareholders and providing them access to a greater role in major corporate decisions.
- Committed to cutting energy and fuel subsides.
- Signaled it is pursuing inclusion in internationally held emerging market bond indices.

However, it is unclear whether the changes will be effective at bolstering confidence, from within or from without, and whether any change will structurally improve crucial institutions. Emblematic of the Egyptian political scene, there is a diversity of voices clamoring for influence at this critical time. But one strong voice comes from the Egyptian Center for Public Policy Studies (ECPPS), which has an impressive track record of not just operating within such turmoil but affecting real policy change amidst it.

The Project

The tumultuous social environment in Egypt presents opportunity for change, but it also creates a lot of noise to filter through. Seeing that a problem exists is a cursory first step; grasping the nuance of reality in a way that translates to affecting progress is the real key. While ECPPS' broad goal is to improve society, it decided to accomplish that end by investigating the core drivers that restrict economic liberties and targeting them for reform.

To determine these pivotal areas, ECPPS partnered with two organizations with robust experience in economic evaluation, the Fraser Institute and Atlas Network. Specifically, they launched an Economic Freedom Audit (EFA). This project would not only trace the root of Egypt's economic woes, but it would provide a roadmap to greater freedom and prosperity.

About ECPPS

The Egyptian Center for Public Policy Studies (ECPPS) is a relatively young think tank, but it already has an accomplished past. It is the successor to the Egyptian Union of Liberal Youth (EULY), which was founded in 2007 to build a cultural movement in Egypt that values freedom. More than half of Egypt's population is below the age of 25, so reaching young people is of paramount importance to affect social change. EULY's ambitious mission was to not only spread liberal ideas to young people in the country but also bring them together and build appreciation for the fruit of liberal culture, such as art, literature, and representative politics.

In 2009, Atlas Network awarded EULY with the Templeton Freedom Award for Excellence in Promoting Liberty for its essay contest, which addressed the prompt, "Why Am I a Liberal?" The initiative was featured by six major newspapers, a youth radio station, and two major Egyptian political parties. It was in 2011 that EULY metamorphized into a think tank—ECPPS—in order to create a greater impact on Egyptian society at large.

The mission of ECPPS is to propose public policies aimed at reforming the legal and economic system in Egypt, promoting the principles of free markets, limited government, individual freedom, and rule of law. ECPPS provides evidence-based research to advocate for legal reforms and public policies in the economic, civil, and political spheres. They use their earned influence to continuing pressing the country toward freedom and reform.

Before beginning the audit, ECPPS sought a thorough appraisal of both Egypt's current standing and how to conduct a successful EFA. They initiated a rigorous review of the five main EFW categories and the 42 subindicators, drawing on specialized material provided by Fraser. They also reviewed other organizations that had completed successful EFAs. Following this investigation, ECPPS narrowed the scope of the EFA to specifically target four leveraged subcomponents of the *EFW* index: intellectual property, nontariff trade barriers, monetary and fiscal policies, and subsidies.

The four policy themes emerged as areas ripe for tangible reforms that could dramatically ameliorate Egypt's steep decline in economic freedom while resonating with enough groups within society that change could be possible. Once ECPPS identified the targeted policy areas, they created a research plan to build substance for their proposals. The specific outputs included research papers for each of the four target areas.

Challenge: Standing Out Among the Crowd

Competing reform initiatives could jeopardize the influence of ECPPS' proposals. At the time of the audit, Egypt was already in the process of undergoing economic reforms under the direction of the IMF. Instead of competition, however, ECPPS viewed this as an opportunity to magnify their impact. The circumstance allowed them to both review progress and suggest areas for improvement for the government to focus on, tailored by their own localized expertise. Their ideas, then, could be viewed as supplements or even compliments to the existing reform efforts.

For the in-person audit workshops, ECPPS identified stakeholders with direct connections to the identified areas. Then they needed to reach out to them.

ECPPS already had an established database of contacts, which allowed them to quickly identify primary contacts to invite. This freed them up to spend time generating a tiered outreach plan to reach additional stakeholders with whom they had not had prior interactions. ECPPS sent invitations to embassies, ministries, governmental bodies, political parties, public figures, and even some international organizations like the World Bank and USAID. They also implemented a social media campaign for outreach activities. And they extended personal invitations over the phone to specific people they deemed vital to the audit.

> **Challenge: Getting the Right People at the Table**
> The success of the EFA hinged on the stakeholders ECPPS was able to engage, as they are the ones positioned to usher reforms into practice. This is one of the most important obstacles think tanks must surmount. ECPPS' success was directly related to the soft power and personal connections their organization had. They had built trust with multiple social circles within their community based on years of quality work and outreach, so they were well positioned for engaging others in the EFA. However, even with its extensive network and friendly relationships, some stakeholder segments were still hard to reach, especially representatives from certain government agencies. It is impossible to reach every intended audience, but by developing a strong outreach plan, ECPPS had built-in contingencies to ensure they gathered crucial and comprehensive feedback.

The initial EFA conference was held on July 30, 2018, at the Golden Tulip Flamenco Hotel in Zamalek. It was well attended by representatives from all the targeted groups. Stakeholders included a member of Parliament (MP) on the Planning and Budget Committee, an MP on the Economic Committee, the Founder and Chairman of the Terous Misr Foundation for Development, the Deputy Minister of Finance, the Chief of the Central Administration of Authorized Economic Operations of the Egyptian Customs Authority, and the Head of the Egyptian Patent Office. The event was also covered in various media outlets, which was one of ECPPS' priorities in reaching the public with their reform proposals.

ECPPS staff designed a communications strategy to elevate the reach of the EFA results following the conference. The outreach plan includes meetings with civic leaders, the public, one-on-one meetings with MPs, and workshops for MP staffers. Meetings with government officials are specifically focused on Egypt's ranking in the target areas, the merits of reform, and the proposed solutions for reform. While the conference was held in July 2018, it is already evident that there is an appetite for the reform measures ECPPS identified.

Zooming In: Building Credibility through Tailored Content

The unique circumstances in Egypt posed an interesting challenge to ECPPS' EFA. Given the country's long history of clashing viewpoints and competing factions, and the acute sensitivities of the stakeholders regarding attempts to influence, the ways in which ECPPS conveyed its message may have been more important than the message itself.

Egyptians are inherently skeptical of anyone promising to fix their problems, because that has often resulted in the opposite. Yet they are at a crossroads and face a plethora of policy options, increasing the importance credibly presenting any proposal for reform. Knowing this in advance, the team focused significant attention on crafting presentations that fostered inclusivity and bolstered credibility.

This is clearly seen in the format of the introductory session of the EFA conference. The session was split between three individuals: Ahmed Ragab, Executive Director of ECPPS; Fred McMahon of the Fraser Institute; and Ahmed Abd El-Wahab, Head of Economic Research at ECPPS.

Ragab, a visible researcher and thought leader, kicked off the event by listing a sampling of economic problems facing Egypt that were well known by audience members. This included the large amount of economic activity in the informal sector, the large budget deficit, the obstacles in creating capital, and inflation. He also noted that Egypt's economic reforms—those led by the IMF—have put Egypt on the road to recovery. The initial speech set the tone for the event and fostered a sense of community and shared purpose among the attendees.

McMahon's segment presented the goal of the EFA: to identify policy reforms that will lead to economic growth, prosperity, and inclusive political institutions. He provided examples of economically free countries—like Botswana, Ireland, Singapore, and South Korea—that Egyptians would recognize and be attracted to emulate. He used data from the Fraser Institute to offer empirical evidence to support his claims and gain credibility with the audience.

The last portion, led by Abd El-Wahab, provided the audience with a roadmap for the later sessions and the EFA in general. He introduced the four policy areas targeted for reform, drawing on his expertise as ECPPS's head economic researcher to lend further credibility to their strategy. He explained that ECPPS would conduct the research, host a series of conversations with stakeholders and leaders, and promote the policy recommendations. This conveyed local ownership of the reforms being pursued.

Each presenter revealed a particular strength that contributed to the credibility of the program, while presenting in concert quelled reservations against outsider influence.

The opening conference is a key point in an EFA because it is the best shot at getting everyone on the same page, a feat that can return benefits throughout the entire project. Attendees arrive with different backgrounds, skill sets, and knowledge. To bolster the efficacy of the EFA, ECPPS addressed the asymmetrical knowledge of participants in a way that generated more effective and efficient discussion. Their strategy involved:

- Establishing a shared sense of community
- Presenting the goal and eliciting cooperation
- Including the audience in the solution.

Key Insights

A unique challenge for ECPPS was uniting disparate interests toward a common goal. Due to their tumultuous history, many Egyptians are wary of calls to reform. And yet, those same people see the prosperity of other nations and desire to engage in the global economy and realize their own potential. This presents a narrow opportunity for sound policy ideas to be adopted when articulated clearly and with credibility.

ECPPS internalized the cultural tension into the entire EFA project. It drew on the common knowledge that policy change is imminent, reinforcing what the public and civic leaders have seen in media headlines. Then it provided a channel for others to participate in the solution. By providing clearly defined policy reform proposals that resonate with the daily struggles of everyday people, and backing them up with sound data and citations in media, ECPPS has fostered the image of a passionate, credible, and action-ready public advocate.

A successful audit can lead to serious policy changes and ideological shifts, so determining the factors that ensure success of an EFA is crucial. From ECPPS's experience, a number of important lessons arise. First, ECPPS recognized the unique economic position of its country. If there is any time to push toward economic freedom, this is it. Important, sympathetic ears are currently open to suggestions, exemplified by numerous attendees that were high-level government employees. Second, ECPPS utilized the experience of its network to reach these Egyptian leaders. Third, ECPPS used its introductory conference to create an efficient, informed atmosphere—one crucial to the success of an EFA.

Although the EFA is currently ongoing, ECPPS's audit can become the groundwork for more sustained, substantial change in Egypt. ECPPS plans to use its EFA to examine current reforms while also proposing new ones, striking while the iron is hot.

Discussion Questions

- What enabled ECPPS to expand its outreach to contacts beyond its social network?
- What natural endowment constraints or historical inertia does your organization face?

- How can international organizations help or hinder efforts to advance policies supporting economic freedom?
- What are the cultural tensions in your country that impact the policy proposals that are possible? How could these tensions shift? How can you work around (or through) them?
- What are the advantages (and disadvantages) of targeting a specific age demographic with either certain programs or the organization's mission?
- How does social change occur in your country? How are your programs equipped to navigate those channels of change? How are you ill-equipped to do so?
- How has your organization pushed the boundaries of what is politically possible? What have you learned from that process? How did you internalize lessons learned into the organization?

How to Use This Book
Guidance for Think Tank Teams

The primary purpose of this publication is to disseminate among our network of think tank partners useful examples of impressive think tank projects. However, Atlas Network does not suggest think tanks try to replicate these projects uncritically.

Rather, the case studies in this volume should be used to prompt interesting discussions among think tank teams as they develop their own visions for change. For each case study, suggested discussion questions are included that can help guide those conversations. In this way, we see the key value in case studies as providing a shared starting point for ambitious and creative thinking.

At the same time, there are many opportunities to avoid "reinventing the wheel," and we have found that most think tank partners are more than willing to cooperate with other organizations who express interest in doing similar work and who would like to replicate some aspects of the original project. Of course, any reader should be sure to communicate their intentions and seek permission from the subject wherever appropriate.

Below is just one suggested set of exercises for teams interesting in using the enclosed case studies for brainstorming.

Step One: Identify one to three case studies for your entire team to read, and assign the reading to be completed by a specified time. Note that all case studies in this book are available as separate downloads at AtlasNetwork.org/training.

Step Two: Schedule a brainstorming discussion with one or two specific organizational priorities in mind and communicate those to the team. For example, your organization may be planning a new research project on the topic of trade. Ask the team to be thinking about that project and the project goals as they read the assigned case studies.

Step Three: When you convene, decide who is going to be the scribe to keep track of the comments. Then, establish a few ground rules for the brainstorm and have the scribe write them somewhere everyone can see them throughout the brainstorm. Some typical rules include:

- Speak one at a time.
- Do not speak too much or too little. Each person should contribute their views to make sure every voice is included.
- Do not spend any time at this stage disagreeing with each other. The purpose of brainstorming is to bring as many ideas to the surface as possible, and time will quickly expire if you spend it responding to each other's comments. This can also have the effect of discouraging openness and honesty.
- Invite the team to suggest additional ground rules they would like observed during the brainstorm.

Step Four: Identify at least three open-ended questions for the group to respond to using the case studies as reference material. Depending on group size, you may elect to break up into teams of three or four to work on the answers together and then report back to the larger group after 20–30 minutes. Some sample questions include:

- From the case studies we read prior to this brainstorm, what are some useful insights we can apply to our upcoming project?
- What opportunities do we have to do things differently to increase our chances of success on our upcoming project?
- What are some unique aspects of our local context that we will need to account for in our planning?
- What are we doing well as an organization that we should take care to preserve and/or nurture?
- What are some challenges that, if we could overcome them, would really help our organization go to the next level of success?

Step Five: Have the scribe summarize and review the feedback with the team, and then be sure to give the group a chance to clarify anything that was misinterpreted or omitted.

Step Six: Finally, discuss what some specific next steps might be. Many times this need not represent any irrevocable decisions made during the brainstorm but further discussion such as:

- The research and communications teams are going to meet once a week to develop a marketing plan for the upcoming project.
- Key board members are going to be solicited for their input on one or two key questions that arose during the meeting.
- Leadership is going to consider a new hire or contractor to fill a critical skill gap needed for the upcoming project.

For exercises like this, leadership should demonstrate genuine interest in team members' input, recognizing that "people support what they help create." This approach need not interfere with a leader's desire to preserve ultimate decision-making authority. For this reason, it is suggested that brainstorm meetings not include the expectation that big decisions will be made during the meeting but rather that the input will be used to inform those decisions as appropriate and when feasible.

Most teams understand that not every point of view can be accommodated, but a genuine desire on the part of leadership to be made aware of those views and to consider those views authentically is a productive way to ensure all of the knowledge in the organization is being brought to bear on important decisions.

About Atlas Network

Mission

Atlas Network increases opportunity and prosperity by strengthening a global network of independent civil society organizations that promote individual freedom and remove barriers to human flourishing.

Overarching Strategy

Atlas Network cultivates a network of partners that share a vision of a free, prosperous, and peaceful world where the rule of law, private property, and free markets are defended by governments whose powers are limited. To accelerate the pace of achievement by its partners in their local communities, Atlas Network implements programs within its *Coach, Compete, Celebrate* strategic model.

- *Coach* Atlas Network provides world-class training and mentoring to inspire professionalism and improve performance among its independent partners.
- *Compete* Atlas Network offers grant and prize competitions that fuel its partners' efforts to achieve extraordinary outcomes.
- *Celebrate* Atlas Network fosters camaraderie and stokes ambitions among its partners by celebrating their greatest accomplishments through its events and media outreach.

About Doing Development Differently

Atlas Network joins the many other scholars, practitioners, and activists who support the movement to start Doing Development Differently. For our part, we offer our unique strategy of combining a

185

commitment to increased economic freedom and supporting a local vision for change. Using our network of 485 local think tanks, we pursue increased economic opportunities for low-income populations by supporting projects that seek to strengthen core government institutions—property rights, rule of law, free markets—and remove institutional barriers that make it difficult for people in poor places to succeed. To learn more, visit AtlasNetwork.org/Difference.

About the Publication Team

Matt Warner is President of Atlas Network. Under the direction of the CEO, he is responsible for strategy, programming, and personnel management. Matt also leads the development of a research agenda to further demonstrate the invaluable role of think tanks in achieving freedom around the world. Matt writes, speaks, and consults internationally on the topics of economics, institution building, nonprofit management, measurement, and impact philanthropy.

Matt coined the term "the outsider's dilemma" to describe the challenge of helping low-income countries develop without inadvertently and perversely getting in the way of their most viable paths to prosperity. His work has appeared in *Cato Journal*, *Forbes*, Harvard's *Education Next*, Real Clear Markets, Foundation for Economic Education, EconTalk, and the *Washington Times*, among others. Prior to joining Atlas Network in 2010, Matt served in various policy leadership positions at nonprofit think tanks with a focus on energy, education, and property rights.

Matt has a master's degree in economics from George Mason University and is certified by Georgetown University in organizational development consulting. He is also a member of American Enterprise Institute's Leadership Network, a Penn Kemble Fellow with the National Endowment for Democracy, and a recipient of America's Future Foundation's 2019 Buckley Award. Matt and his wife Chrissy, an attorney, live in Vienna, Virginia, with their four children.

Casey Pifer is the Director of Institute Relations at Atlas Network. She manages the grants and awards programs of Atlas Network, including the prestigious Templeton Freedom Award. Originally from West Virginia, Casey joined Atlas Network in 2014 on the events team but has since transitioned to her current position. She grew up in West Virginia and graduated from West Virginia University with a bachelor's degree in economics and political science.

Melissa Mann joined Atlas Network as Director of Partnerships in 2018 and became the Vice President of Communications in 2019. Prior to joining Atlas Network, Melissa spent seventeen years as Director of Development at Reason Foundation, a public policy and media organization that advances a free society by developing, applying, and promoting libertarian principles, including individual liberty, free markets, and the rule of law. She is a 2016 graduate of Atlas Network's Think Tank MBA program.

Melissa received a bachelor's degree in Diplomacy and World Affairs from Occidental College in Los Angeles and did graduate work in public policy and law at the Universität des Saarlandes in Saarbrücken and Rheinische-Friedrich-Wilhelms-Universität Bonn, both in what was then West Germany. From her home in Los Angeles, Melissa spends her free time reading liberty-themed nonfiction; doing voiceovers for commercials, videogames, and telephone answering systems; and chasing peacocks around her backyard.

AJ Skiera first joined Atlas Network in 2016. He attended the University of Miami (FL) with a semester abroad at Charles University in Prague, where he graduated summa cum laude with a bachelor's degree in history and political science. In his role as Associate Director of Marketing and Communications, he helps to craft and facilitate Atlas Network's content strategy across email, web, print, video, and social media platforms.

AJ is managing Atlas Network's photojournalism and film project for its Doing Development Differently initiative, which features real stories of individuals who are the downstream beneficiaries of free-market reforms successfully championed by Atlas Network's most effective partners in Latin America, Asia, and Europe. He is a graduate of three professional development programs with the Charles Koch Institute and a recipient of the Illinois State Society Scholarship for his time working for Congressman Randy Hultgren (IL-14). Originally from the northwest suburbs of Chicago, he currently resides in Arlington, Virginia.

Learn More

Books

Why Nations Fail, Daron Acemoglu and James Robinson
Building State Capability, Matt Andrews, Lant Pritchett,
   Michael Woolcock
The Origin of Wealth, Erick Beinhocker
Doing Bad by Doing Good, Chris Coyne
The Great Escape, Angus Deaton
Tyranny of Experts, William Easterly
How Change Happens, Duncan Green
The Atlas of Economic Complexity, Richard Hausmann
Navigation by Judgment, Dan Honig
The Alternative, Mauricio Miller
Dead Aid, Dambisa Moyo
The Idealist, Nina Munk
The Bright Continent, Dayo Olopade
The Power of Positive Deviance, Richard Pascale, Jerry Sternin,
   Monique Sternin
Aid on the Edge of Chaos, Ben Ramalingam
Development and Freedom, Amartya Sen
Why We Lie About Aid, Pablo Yanguas

Videos

Stories of Impact
PovertyandFreedom.org

Made in Mékhé
FEE.org

Poverty, Inc.
PovertyInc.org

Resources

Global Directory of Think Tanks
AtlasNetwork.org/Directory

Case Studies Online
AtlasNetwork.org/Case-studies

Events

AtlasNetwork.org/Events